God Gave Me A Dream

Norman Barnes

As told to
Rod Boreham

CW00607398

New Wine Press

© 1988 Rod Boreham

New Wine Ministries,
P.O. Box 17,
Chichester,
West Sussex   PO20 6RY

All rights reserved. No part of this publication may be re-
produced, stored in a retrieval system or transmitted in any
form or by any means, mechanical, electronic, photocopy-
ing or otherwise without the prior written consent of the
publisher.
Short extracts may be quoted for review purposes.
Bible quotations are taken from the Holy Bible, New International Version.
Copyright © 1973, 1978 International Bible Society.
Published by Hodder & Stoughton.

ISBN 0 947852 45 X

Contents

Foreword

A 'chance' engagement found me speaking at the local Pentecostal church's weekly youth meeting. The person booked to share had been taken ill and I was asked to stand in at the last moment. The handful of young people gathered gave me their eager attention and as I started to minister numbers suddenly doubled when a group of black christians piled in through the back door. My subject was 'Take the whole armour of God!' At the close I called for a fresh commitment to the service of Jesus and almost the whole meeting responded. I thought revival had broken out.

In the midst of all the prayer and shouts of praise was a young man weeping and crying out to the Lord for blessing as he dedicated himself to world mission. That young man was Norman Barnes and that meeting began almost thirty years of friendship and working together to date. It's not been without its hiccups, as you'll read, but I am profoundly grateful to Jesus that he caused our paths to cross and I believe the 'best is yet to come.'

In all those years Norman, and his lovely wife Grace, have not lost their hunger to see God move in power. They have never visibly wavered in their zeal to see precious people won to Jesus. Their concern for the needy world has only increased as they have travailed, ministered and journeyed to country after country. With the passage of time, to Norman's youth and enthusiasm, God has added faithfulness and wisdom and he has emerged as a modern pioneer and statesman in the cause of bridge-building and mission.

From the beach at Brighton to the more distant shores of Africa and Asia; from London's Soho to Hong Kong and beyond; from suburban mission hall to star-studded Texas, two words shine through in Norman's life, 'faith' and 'vision'. Without any ballyhoo or sentiment I'm proud to have Norman as my friend and know of no-one better to encourage you with tears and smiles to make your dreams come true.

JOHN NOBLE

Introduction

11,000 young people attended Mission '87, a five day youth congress held in Utrecht, The Netherlands, and organised by T.E.M.A. (The European Missionary Alliance). Time and time again throughout the five days the challenge went out loud and clear to consider the call to evangelism and world mission. For many the Congress was a life altering experience as they surrendered to the call to serve God.

Day four was the one and only meeting for each national group. Around 600 people gathered for the British meeting. It was noisy in the hall, for behind the platform was a very flimsy partition, beyond which another meeting was taking place for a different national grouping. As Norman Barnes, Director of Links International and Vice Chairman of the T.E.M.A. national committee stood to speak, all he could hear behind him was the noise from the other meeting. He had no way of knowing just how much that noise could be heard by those attending the British meeting, or if the P.A. system he was about to use would be adequately powerful. The last thing he wanted was for people to be straining to hear what he had to say, or indeed go away from the meeting not having heard anything. Norman decided that there was only one thing to do to be absolutely sure about the whole matter. He had a message to give that he believed to be from God and so in order to overcome all the noise he simply stood at the microphone and attempted to shout over the top of the unavoidable din.

He poured out his heart to the young people listening intently to what he had to say. He told them how so many people get trapped by the concept of the will of God as a rigid, narrow, inflexible matter. Well meaning, enthusiastic and sincere people who are desirous of giving all they have and are in service to God, often are prevented from doing just that, because they are unsure whether it really is the will

7

of God for them to undertake some sort of service, whether at home or abroad. As a result many lives are wasted and the Kingdom of God suffers.

"Everyone of us" he said, "have been given dreams. We all have longings in our hearts to do something, to be something for God. The problem is, many of us do not realise that those dreams that we cherish have been put there by the Holy Spirit and he wants to see them become reality. Don't get all hung up about whether the thing you want to do is the will of God or not. Has God put a dream in your heart? What is it that you long to accomplish? Make your dream a reality. Tell someone about it, confess it to the Lord, pray about it and then look to God to open up the way for you."

At the close of his message, he asked people to gather in small groups and pray together about their dreams, asking God to establish them firmly in their lives. All around the hall hopes and aspirations began to be expressed, and not a few tears were shed as young people realised that the longings of their hearts were not merely fantasy and could actually become reality for them.

In the counselling room after the meeting there were a number of positive responses, with enquiries along the lines of what people could actually do about the dreams they held; a problem that any congress or mission is happy to have.

Each national grouping also had to fill in a response card for the whole event, and a number mentioned the fact that the national meeting where the speaker talked about dreams was the highlight for them.

There were one or two very negative responses to Norman's ministry. They mistook his shouting for raving and felt he had gone on an ego trip. Such is life for enthusiastic communicators!

Misunderstanding is nothing new to Norman. A man who dreams big dreams himself and works to see them fulfilled will inevitably be misunderstood. His enthusiasm will sometimes be regarded as being pushy and his determination be mistaken for bigheadedness. His zeal may sometimes make people think he lacks sensitivity and his success will either cause admiration or jealousy. Norman has encountered all of these reactions, but still continues to dream and see his dreams fulfilled.

When he stood to speak at Mission '87, it was just one more fulfilment. An opportunity to share with young people about a few of the opportunities available to those who are prepared to go for the sake of the Gospel, and see many responding to the challenge was just one more desire that he had held in his heart.

This is the story of two dreamers, Norman and Grace Barnes, ordinary people from east London who dared to believe some of the incredible things God spoke to them about and who, through much joy, considerable sorrow and the miraculous and caring hand of their heavenly Father, have watched His purposes unfold for their lives, bringing blessing to themselves, and many, many others.

ROD BOREHAM

Chapter 1
The World in my Heart

People with a vision but no task may be labelled dreamers, but those who have a task and no vision will almost certainly live a life of boredom and drudgery. There is nothing more soul-destroying and frustrating than carrying out work for which there seems no real purpose; labour for which there would be little return in the way of personal fulfilment.

If I had to choose between the two groups, I know to which I would rather belong. I have always been a dreamer, always had hope in my heart that certain things would happen, and have done my best to pursue those dreams.

A dreamer is frowned upon in our culture. The term is usually associated with somebody who has got their head in the clouds; they are living in a world of unreality; always dreaming of what might be, rather than getting on with the here and now. And there may well be people like that, who only dream but never actually do anything about seeing their dreams become reality. Those who want their dreams to come true have certainly got to wake up!

Nothing of any significance has been achieved in the world without someone first dreaming of it happening. Whether it was an architect working on a revolutionary design for a building; a scientist seeking a cure for a killer disease; missionaries wanting to set up schools, hospitals and churches in some corner of the globe as yet unreached by the Gospel of Christ; or a married couple longing for a family. So many of the achievements and events in our lives start off as a seed thought that slowly fills our hearts and minds and becomes a vision worth pursuing, a goal to strive for.

Many of the noteworthy characters, people who made an

impression on the society in which they lived, would have been regarded as dreamers. The words of Martin Luther King ring loudly in my ears. ''I have a dream'' he declared to the thousands who gathered to hear him speak. Those words spoken so confidently, that inspired many, are etched with sadness now, when one remembers how dearly that great man paid for his dream. Knowing, however, that his life was on the line most of the time, did not stop him from pursuing his dream and taking practical steps to see it fulfilled.

Dreams, however, are not just for the 'great'. We all cherish hopes, desires and ambitions in our hearts which will be as diverse as we are. There are very few human beings who do not dream of achieving something in life, or improving themselves and their lot in some way. Some of those dreams could be very selfish and it might even be better if they were never fulfilled. On the other hand, more of our dreams than we care to imagine are placed in our hearts by a loving Father who wants His children to reach out, take hold of them and make them reality.

Almost from the moment I became a Christian at the age of 16 years old, God put a vision in my heart to reach the world. In retrospect, it must have seemed ludicrous to those who knew about my dream. Who did this young lad from Dagenham, Essex, think he was, believing that the Lord had spoken to him about touching and helping to meet some of the crying needs of our world? But believe, I did; even though I had no real conception of what this meant. All I knew was, I could not be content until I saw this dream fulfilled.

The youth group to which I belonged at Dagenham Elim Church was experiencing some extraordinary times of blessing. The Holy Spirit seemed to be doing a special work in the lives of the members of the group, which strangely did not seem to be touching the rest of the Church. On a number of occasions that we met the presence of God seemed to fill

12

the room in such a tangible way, that we found ourselves prostrated on the floor. The subject of being slain in the Spirit is a regular item for discussion in the current move of the Holy Spirit around the world, but in 1958 we simply referred to it as being flat on our faces before the Lord.

On one such occasion we met to seek the Lord. We were full of expectancy, young people with a burning desire to serve the Lord and know His power work in and through us. I was standing, praying, when the Holy Spirit touched me. My knees buckled and I found myself on my face before the Lord. For a period of about 2 hours all I could do was speak in tongues, but as I did this, I became aware of a vision so real, I felt that I could have reached out and touched it. The scene being portrayed before my eyes was so vivid, I felt as if I had been transported bodily out of the small meeting room to where this scene was taking place.

I could see myself on an elevated platform in a large building, preaching. As I spoke in tongues, so what I was saying seemed to correspond with what I heard myself preaching in the vision. I moved around on the platform, and looked out on a sea of black faces. I could see thousands of black people listening intently to what I had to say. As I preached, they responded eagerly to my words and at the close of the message I gave an appeal. Many came forward to the platform as a result to meet with God, and at that point the vision faded.

I was thrilled and deeply moved by what I had experienced. It took me some time to come back to reality. I knew somehow that what I had seen was a vision of a place in Africa and as I 'came round' I looked at the twenty or so other young people in the room. "Have I been here all the time?" I asked.

"Yes, of course you have," they assured me, slightly amused by the fact that I should even ask.

I explained what had happened to me. With the sort of confidence that only comes with youth I stated clearly, "one

13

day God will get me to Africa.'' The look of incredulity on everyone's faces was enough to convince me that most of them were not as confident about the fact as I was. The leader of the meeting, Charles Calvert, had become a good friend to me and seemed to appreciate me. ''You believe it Norman,'' he said, ''and one day God will get you there.''

Those words were a great encouragement and gave me renewed enthusiasm and a trust in God to perform what he had shown me, even if no one else in the room believed me.

With hindsight I can see that it must have been difficult for them to accept what I was saying without any shadow of doubt. I was a bit of a loud-mouth and thought a lot of myself, and my statement must have sounded arrogant to say the least. But along with this less acceptable side of my nature, I did have a deep desire to serve God and was willing to undertake almost any task I was asked to do. Under the circumstances it might have been wiser to wait for a while before I shared with the rest of the group about the vision.

Joseph is one character in the Bible that I admire. Time and time again he literally bounced back from the pits, the depths of despair, eventually to rise to a position of immense power in Egypt and thus become the saviour of his family in a time of famine. But it required a lot of hard dealings by the Lord before his character was formed enough to cope with such an elevated position.

As a young man, he was his father's favourite. This undoubtedly caused jealousy amongst his brothers, and the gift of a rather expensive coat did nothing to endear him further to them. He also received dreams from time to time, and, whether out of naivety, youthful exuberance or wishing to be provocative is not clear, he wasted no time in sharing his dreams with his brothers. Which would have caused no problem, but for the nature of the dreams.

''I dreamt'' he announced one day, ''that we were binding sheaves of corn out in the field, when suddenly my sheaf rose and stood upright, while your sheaves gathered round mine and bowed down to it. And I had another dream, and this time the sun and moon and eleven stars were bowing down to me.'' His family had no problem in interpreting the dreams and, needless to say, were less than overwhelmed by these proclamations. Hardly surprising and not very wise on Joseph's part. But I can identify with him. God had spoken to him quite clearly through the dreams, and before he had given any time to think about the repercussions, had blurted out the whole scenario. I feel sure, in spite of his brothers' reactions and all the subsequent events in his life, those dreams remained very real to him.

After the vision I received about Africa, I knew beyond all doubt that the dream God had put in my heart about reaching the world was going to be fulfilled. I felt confident that I would serve the Lord full-time and I would travel the world in the course of my ministry. The vision only served to confirm all those feelings, but like Joseph, I was sometimes insensitive as to when and how I shared these things. I cannot blame people for thinking that I was a big-head at the time.

Patience was also not very high on my list of virtues. I never doubted that God would perform what he had shown me, but I had one problem, I wanted him to do it immediately. I wrestled with him about it, plagued him, agonised over it, desperately wanting to see some action. The Lord was very gracious to me and spoke to me with these words, ''After you have received the promise, wait patiently.''

Joseph must have thought he had made it when he was appointed as chief servant in Potiphar's house. After the treachery by his brothers, he had good reason to believe that things were finally going to work out better. Maybe those dreams he had were closer to reality than ever, after all, he had a position of responsibility, and compared with his brothers, he was a man of some importance.

But we all know what happened. Refusing to have anything to do with Potiphar's wife's advances and suggestions was the cause of another downfall. He had avoided sin and yet had been cast as the villain of the piece and put in jail. How excited he must have been when he was first given a job in Potiphar's house. How crestfallen he must have felt when his act of righteousness only seemed to take him a giant step backwards and down the social ladder, in fact to below the bottom rung. The questions must have plagued him. "How could this happen? I only did what was right. Why did God allow this?"

God used the situation to further his purposes for Joseph's life, develop the man's character and continue moulding him into the person he wanted him to be.

People who actively pursue their dreams and are impatient to see them come true, are prone to try and make things happen. Like Joseph, they find themselves making one or two false starts. Five years after I had received the vision about Africa, during which time the longing to see the vision fulfilled never left me, I thought the moment had come.

On a number of occasions I had been thrilled by films from the T.L. Osborn Evangelistic Association. They showed meetings held by the evangelist in different countries around the world, with vast crowds in attendance. Hundreds of people committed their lives to Christ and many miracles of healing were recorded. A film about such meetings in Ghana challenged and stirred me in particular. I could almost feel myself on the platform like T.L. Osborn, preaching to thousands of Africans. Imagine my excitement and sense of anticipation when an opportunity arose to meet the U.K. representative of the T.L. Osborn organisation. My mind ran riot! At last the door of opportunity was about to open. I was on my way to Africa!

I met the representative and told him of all my dreams and plans and how I was convinced God wanted me to go to Africa. I ws given an invitation to join the organisation, and my understanding was that this would eventually lead me to Africa. For the time being, however, they wanted me to travel around the U.K. showing films and generally promoting the work of the T.L. Osborn Evangelistic Association.

I left the meeting with the representative with hopes flying high. At last I felt something was really beginning to happen. Within a very short space of time, however, my enthusiasm began to dampen and a growing sense of unease about the whole proposal began to grip me. The question of financial support for the work I was to underake was unclear. I had also become engaged to Grace and I was unsure how this work would affect our relationship. These two factors, plus an overriding sense that I was actually pre-empting what God wanted to do, made me think again. Not long after, the proposals were dropped. God had put the world in my heart but he showed me that I would get to Africa in my own right. I was not to keep on trying to engineer the situation.

In spite of the fact that I knew this was right, I couldn't help feeling disappointed, but by this time I was involved in a ministry team called the 'Good News Team' as well as carrying out gainful employment in a Merchant Bank. I diverted all my energies into whatever opportunities for ministry came my way. Regularly, at weekends, the team would make its way to a designated place to preach in the open air. In summer, this would mostly take place at one of the coastal resorts, and we regularly preached to hundreds of people. It was nothing unusual to see members of the crowd weeping as we witnessed to them and it was a great thrill to lead many to a place of surrender to the Lord Jesus Christ.

Dreaming of Miracles

While I was involved with the ministry team, another dream began to come to birth in my heart. Often, whilst travelling together I would sit with a man named Les Hilary. Whenever he broke bread he would say "thank you Lord for another week of perfect health". They were not just idle words, for he was a real testimony to divine health. I was greatly challenged by Les' attitude and began to seek God about the whole area of healing. I became aware of the importance of seeing the Gospel demonstrated in signs and wonders and not just preached. I began to see that the evangelistic ministry needed accompanying signs and miracles in order for people to know that God is indeed the Lord. I saw how important Jesus regarded the miracles that he did, not only in actually meeting people's needs, but in revealing who he was. It was through a miracle that the disciples first came to put their faith in him. After he had performed the famous, and for the host of the wedding reception, face-saving miracle of turning water into wine, we read the following words: *"This, the first of his miraculous signs Jesus performed in Cana of Galilee. He thus revealed his glory, and his disciples put their faith in him."* (John 2 v 11).

It began to dawn on the disciples who Jesus was after they saw this amazing manifestation of the power of God.

On another occasion, when Jesus was talking to the crowds, there were a number of religious leaders present displaying their usual cynicism and unbelief. Jesus was trying to explain who he was and how he was one with the Father. It seems to me that almost in frustration at the hardness of their hearts, he says *"Do not believe me unless I do what my Father does. But if I do it, even though you do not believe me, believe the miracles that you may learn and understand that the Father is in me, and I in the Father."*

I longed to see a manifestation of God's healing power in a way that would make people really sit up and take notice. I was grateful for the isolated incidents that we witnessed, but I knew that when I looked at the life of Jesus and the early Church, there was so much more of God's power available than the Church of today seemed able to appropriate.

I found myself easily moved at the sight of suffering. Just seeing someone in a wheelchair moved me to tears. The films of T.L. Osborn, showing one miracle after another, convinced me that such regular and abundant manifestations were meant to be the norm. I devoured every piece of literature I could find on the subject and prayed constantly, earnestly seeking God for a ministry of healing. One day, quite simply, I felt that God had heard and answered my prayer and that I would see miracles of healing in the way I desired.

I was never afraid to take risks when I thought I had heard from God, even if at times I did move in presumption rather than in faith. I started to pray for sick people in the street. Once, when preaching on a soap-box outside Foyle's Bookshop in London, I declared with utter confidence "God is a God of miracles."

"Do you really believe that?" a man in the crowd shouted back at me.

"Yes" I replied, still full of youthful confidence.

"Do you believe God can heal?" the man persisted.

"Yes, I do."

"Do you think God can heal this?" he asked, holding up his hand.

It was clear that the man's hand was paralysed and could best be described as a claw, such was the rigid position in which the joints of his hand were stuck. I learned later that he had been to hospital and in his pocket was a piece of paper to say that his hand was indeed totally paralysed and there was very little the medical profession could do for him.

I got down from my soap-box and made my way through the crowd to where he stood and prayed for him. As I asked God to heal him, the power of the Holy Spirit came upon him and he began to move his fingers. Within a matter of moments he was jumping up and down, shouting about what had happened, or to put it in scriptural terms, "walking and

19

leaping and praising God". The size of the crowd doubled almost immediately. The moment a miracle took place, people came running. This thrilled and challenged me and was yet more confirmation to me that God wanted to accompany evangelism with signs and wonders.

We continued to see God healing people, but not with the regularity I knew was possible, so I continued to seek God earnestly about this. One thing bothered me. I did not feel comfortable preaching about God's power to heal and seeing people healed, while I wore spectacles. I asked the Lord many times to heal my eyesight.

From my school days I had always had to wear spectacles with very strong lenses. My sight was so poor that when I had an eye test and was asked to read the letters from the card, I could not even see the card!

I felt greatly challenged by this situation. How could I go on proclaiming God's power to heal when I was almost as blind as a bat? Many times I prayed, removed my spectacles, only to find that nothing had happened. I could not come to terms with what seemed to be a total contradiction in my life and to my beliefs.

One evening I sat in a meeting listening to a dear friend called Cecil Cousens ministering on the subject of faith. Once again I became exercised about my eyes. As I lifted my heart to God I felt Him speak to me and say ''now!'' I knew that if I did not obey at that moment I could miss out on healing for my eyes altogether. I removed my spectacles and gave them to Grace, now my wife. The next morning, a Monday, as I woke up, whereas before I could not even see the time on the alarm clock by the bed, now I could see perfectly.

I walked on air to work, my heart full of gratitude to God. Naturally my colleagues asked where my spectacles were. ''God has healed me'' I told them with delight and complete confidence. They tried to suggest all sorts of reasons why I could now suddenly see, but there was no denying what had happened.

All that week I rejoiced in my ability to see everything without the aid of spectacles. On Saturday morning I woke up and could not see the alarm clock. My eye-sight was as bad as it had ever been. I went shopping with Grace to buy her a new pair of boots, and could not even read the price tags. But I refused to put my spectacles back on. I walked round the whole weekend saying "Lord if you can do it for one week, you can do it for good. I claim my healing."

On Monday morning I woke to find my eye-sight perfectly restored again and I never wore glasses again from the age of 22 years to 41 years, and even then it was only for watching T.V. and night driving.

I became a real pain to anyone who wore spectacles. I put them under pressure to seek God and claim healing for their eyesight. My lack of sensitivity was plain to all but myself and I had to learn the hard way that things were not always as simple as I would have liked.

At the age of 25 years I felt God speaking to me again about healing. He told me that the gift of healing would be withdrawn from me for a period of time, and although I was to continue praying for people, I would not experience a spectacular healing ministry in the way I desired, at least not for the time being. Looking back at that moment, I realise the wisdom of God. I could not have been trusted with such a ministry. With my character and personality I would have been unbearable and there were many lessons I had to learn.

I still believe, however, that we will see miracles taking place in profusion. I continue to dream about such a ministry and I am confident it will begin to happen in the not too distant future. In our own fellowship we have seen a good number of people healed of various diseases and illnesses, but this has been through the corporate prayer of God's people, rather than through the healing ministry of one individual.

On a trip to America in 1985, Grace and I were prayed for by a group of ministers who knew nothing about us, and out of the blue one of them prophesied to me that God would begin to fulfil the desires of my heart very soon, with regard to healing. God's idea of soon and mine are not always quite the same of course, but there is no doubt in my heart my dream will come true and I will have the joy of seeing Jesus meet the deepest needs of many people.

Life goes on

Joseph found himself in prison, victim of the unjust treatment and accusations of Potiphar's wife. He could have become bitter, frustrated and angry at a God who had promised so much and yet seemed to have failed to deliver the goods. He could have become withdrawn and enclosed himself in a world of self-pity, but he did not. We read in Genesis 39 v 21-23: *"The Lord was with him; he showed him kindness and granted him favour in the eyes of the prison warder. So the warder put Joseph in charge of all those held in the prison, and he was made responsible for all that was done there. The warder paid no attention to anything under Joseph's care, because the Lord was with Joseph and gave him success in whatever he did."*

Joseph did not give up because his dreams were apparently not being fulfilled. He made use of himself. His attitude was clear and he was available for any responsibility the Lord put his way. He was the exact opposite of the type of people that I mentioned at the beginning of the chapter; dreamers with their heads in the clouds who are totally useless for what is happening here and now. He continued to work with God in and through the circumstances in which he found himself and thus enabled the Lord to work out his purposes in his life.

It is so easy to become down-hearted when you feel those things which God has placed in your heart to pursue, fail to materialise as quickly as you would like. My desire to touch the world's needs and especially see the vision of Africa fulfilled, did not diminish in the slightest, in fact, it only grew. I realised, however, that it was no use sitting around waiting for it to happen, I had to get on with life in the meantime, besides, the desire to serve God in any way was too great for me to want to wait passively, hoping that something would turn up.

Apart from working with the Good News team, I also had opportunities to share my testimony and preach in local churches, which was of great benefit to me. Whether it had the same effect for my listeners, I am unable to say! Grace and I were also working with a team in London amongst the drug addicts in Soho. The drugs craze had really hit the headlines and we were all inspired by the publication of David Wilkerson's book 'The Cross and the Switch Blade'. The work in Soho was also well documented in a book by Keith Bill entitled 'The Needle, the Pill and the Saviour'.

One of the original members of the Good News team was my good friend John Noble. He received an invitation to become the pastor of the Chadwell Christian Mission, a small work situated in Chadwell Heath, on the east side of London, but turned down the offer. We were to learn later that he suggested Grace and I as suitable people for the position. We were eventually approached and after some deliberation, took over responsibility for the work. The additional responsibility involved, including caring for people, counselling, upkeep of the building and outreach, was enough to keep us more than occupied for a good number of years.

My emotions see-sawed during this period when I thought about my dream. At times I felt totally daunted by the fact that the Lord had told me I would reach the world. In my better moments I was totally fulfilled and involved in all that was happening at the Mission. In my worst periods of frustration I would wonder when on earth all that God had spoken to me about was going to happen. How would I ever do it? Time was marching on. I was getting older and nothing of any significance seemed to be happening.

At the same time as Joseph was imprisoned, two of the Pharoah's chief officials were in disgrace and found themselves under his charge. They both had dreams the same night and when they told Joseph that they were a bit dejected because they had no-one to interpret their dreams, Joseph replied "Do not interpretations belong to God? Tell me your dreams."

Although Joseph was able to interpret their dreams correctly, it did him no good, for he was forgotten as soon as, one way or another, both men found their way out of prison. Then came the moment when Pharoah himself had the dream about seven sleek and fat cows and seven ugly and gaunt cows (Genesis 41). He too could find no-one amongst all his magicians and wise men to interpret the dream and eventually Joseph was brought before him. Pharoah made this statement, "I have heard it said of you that when you hear a dream, you can interpret it."

Joseph's reply is quite revealing about the way that God had dealt with him during his years in prison. "I cannot do it - but God will give Pharoah the answer he desires." This answer was virtually the opposite to what he had given to the two officials in prison. Whereas he had acknowledged that God can interpret dreams in the first instance, he does not point the two men to God but to himself as the answer. Before Pharoah he was a changed man. His opening phrase, "I cannot do it" is indicative of the place God had brought him to. He now acknowledged that without the Lord he could do nothing, and nothing would happen unless God did it. He is a changed, humble man.

Everything within me would have loved to have forced the vision of Africa to be fulfilled, but the years spent working and waiting were important preparation. I learned to love, serve and care for people. If I had gone out to Africa, or anywhere else for that matter, without experiencing those years, I would have gone as an evangelist who might have been able to preach the word convincingly, but I would have been totally unsympathetic to the problems, needs and hurts of the people I met.

Stepping into a Dream

Early in 1979 I received a letter from Ghana. A man called Nicholas Andoh had been given my name by a German lady who must have heard me speak on one of my trips to her country. She had told him that if ever he was in need, he should contact me, although I knew nothing about this. Out of the blue this letter arrived with the simple request, ''can you please help us.'' There was no indication as to exactly what help was required, but the implication was financial assistance.

Although my yearnings to go to Africa were stronger than ever, I did not feel any great response to this request, but decided to consult with two friends who were leading another fellowship in the area, whose advice I respected. I met with John Noble and Maurice Smith, who suggested I should write back and be as non-commital as possible.

Within a very short space of time, I received another letter from Nicholas Andoh explaining that he was involved in a work where they had planted three churches in a relatively short space of time. He wanted me to come and see what they were doing and share with them. This time I felt something quicken in my heart and decided to return to John and Maurice and discuss the matter again.

''Nobody knows who this man Nicholas Andoh is'' was John's response. ''I would advise caution Norman. It could be a confidence trick.''

Maurice's reaction was totally the opposite. ''We have restrained these evangelists long enough. It's about time we let them have their head. Let him flap his wings.''

Because I was undecided myself, both points of view sounded valid. We decided, therefore, that finance, the money I would need to get to Ghana and back, should be the indicator whether God was in this situation.

I went home and prayed. Within six weeks I had been given, from different sources and in varying quantities, the sum of £1200 - enough to do what I wanted. It was the largest amount of money I had ever received as a gift and with great excitement I reported back to John and Maurice.

"Go for it" was John's simple word of encouragement. Needless to say, I needed no urging to write back to Nicholas Andoh and tell him I was coming to Ghana to meet him. While I was making final preparations to leave, I heard of a missionary couple from Ghana who were on furlough in Britain and felt I should speak to them about the forthcoming trip. After I had told them the story, they too were a little cautious.

"You don't know who this man is" they said, echoing the previous doubts expressed by John Noble. Concerned that I should find myself in real difficulties once I arrived in Ghana, they gave me the address of The Church of Pentecost in Ghana and of a couple by the name of David and Margaret Mills, Elim Missionaries who had been seconded to the work of the Church of Pentecost. "If you are in a fix, they will help you" they assured me.

The only address that Nicholas Andoh had given me to write to was a P.O. Box number, which I subsequently found out was a sports stadium 180 miles from the capital Accra. When I wrote to Nicholas, I had no idea if my letter would actually reach him, because at that time the Government had totally shut off the country from the outside world due to a currency change-over. No planes were entering or leaving the country and consequently, no post either.

I decided to go ahead, however, and got all the tickets booked, had all the necessary injections and obtained visas.

26

When the situation seemed to be relaxing on the borders of Ghana, I sent a cable to the P.O. Box number saying I was arriving and got on the first plane out of London for Accra. It was only when we were on the plane, however, that all the passengers were informed that the borders had not yet opened up and that we would have to land that night in the neighbouring country of Togo. This certainly confused the situation. All sorts of questions began to race through my mind. Here I was heading half-way across the world, and I was not going to land where I wanted. Had my cable to Nicholas Andoh got through? Would he know of my arrival? If it had got to Ghana would he turn up a day too early to meet me and give up when I did not arrive? It was certainly too late to turn back. I decided my only course of action was to trust everthing to the Lord and see what happened.

The aircraft landed in Lome Airport, Togo, at 6 p.m. in the evening. The vision I had received twenty years previously was burning in my heart, but it had not prepared me for what I was about to experience. As I got off the plane I thought the engines were still running, but then realised that the heat was totally natural. In that melting heat I found I was expected to walk from the plane, along the tarmac, carrying all my own bags to the airport office, being pushed and pulled on all sides by the people jostling to get to the office first. All around were soldiers displaying guns, guarding the airport and watching the passengers very carefully. The contrast between Heathrow and Lome could not have been more marked.

The flight company, KLM, had arranged for all passengers to be put into quality hotels overnight. As I joined the queue in the office, the only other European on the flight, a man, stood behind me.

"Could I share a room with you?" he asked. He looked as if he knew the ropes. "Yes, that's fine with me" I replied.

We checked in at the five star hotel and Jim, the

27

gentleman who was sharing the room with me, suggested that we should go for a meal.

"What do you do for a living?" was my opening question as we sat down to eat. "Sell books" he replied.

"What sort of books?"

"Christian books."

"Are you a Christian then?" I asked, scarcely able to hide my delight.

"Yes".

"So am I."

At that moment God seemed to speak to me with reassurance. "Do not worry son, I am with you."

I got on very well with Jim and told him the story of Nicholas Andoh and the letter I had received. Jim was by no means negative but offered to help if, once I arrived in Ghana, things did not work out.

The following day we took off from Lome and were the first plane-load of people to arrive in Accra for one month. I felt as if I had landed in the middle of total chaos. There was one mad rush to the airport buildings; no-one queued for anything; people were paying bribes in order to get priority treatment and everything seemed to move so slowly on the official's side that my patience was tested to the limit. Every single document that I had was checked; passport, vaccination certificates and visas. Finally, after three checks, I got through Customs and into the airport arrival section. I had made it - at least, I hoped I had. It was now Tuesday and I had been scheduled to arrive on the Monday, would there be anyone to meet me?

Unbeknown to me, of course, Nicholas Andoh had been praying on the Monday that I was due to arrive knowing nothing about my flight plans. As he prayed, the Lord spoke to him and told him to go to his post-box.

"But Lord", he protested, "there has been no mail for weeks."

After a short conversation he decided he had best obey.

Opening the box, he found my cable telling him of my arrival time, Monday evening. By some miracle, even though the borders were still sealed, the cable had got through. He borrowed some money and hitch-hiked down to Accra, arriving Monday night. Of course, I was nowhere to be found, so he waited until the following morning.

I remember scanning the building very carefully, looking at every face, even though I had no idea what Nicholas Andoh would look like. There were not too many white men around, however, so there was an excellent chance I would be found - if Nicholas was there.

Suddenly someone asked, "are you Pastor Barnes?"

"Yes."

"My name is Nicholas."

I was very relieved to see that Nicholas Andoh was actually a real person. I felt slightly strange in the alien environment, bewildered and overawed by the whole situation and was glad and thankful to God that everything seemed to be working out. After one last word with Jim, who checked if all was satisfactory, I followed Nicholas out of the airport, constantly pressed by the crowds of people who wanted to carry my cases for me.

The sights of Accra greeted me as we made for a booking-office to purchase tickets for a bus ride to Nicholas' home in Kumasi. I had previously only seen people carrying objects on their heads in films, now I saw it in the flesh, and I was totally fascinated. The broken roads and open sewers were a sight for sore eyes, as was the broken down shed that acted as the booking-office.

The bus was a true reflection of the state of the booking-office. It had no springs, and everybody's luggage was thrown onto the top along with the goats and chickens. Not deterred by this, we climbed aboard and made our way to the back seat. As the bus moved off, I sat, knees tucked under my chin, dust blowing in all over me. The jolting, jarring journey was an experience not to be forgotten, made

29

all the more vivid by incidents such as the woman who held her baby out of the window to urinate as the bus travelled along.

Eventually, after a long, tiring journey, during which time the only thing I ate was a banana, we arrived in Kumasi. Nicholas Andoh's home was a two-roomed apartment in a run-down tenement block. The conditions, frankly, were terrible. Nicholas, his wife and two children had to survive in two rooms with a minimum of furniture and no bathroom or toilet. There was a toilet along the corridor, but this belonged to the landlord. Because I was a white man, I was allowed to use it, but in fact it had not worked for six months. The family cooked in the community kitchen in the quadrangle of the tenement block, and over the next few days I was to eat anything I was given - something that would have given most Europeans in Ghana the horrors.

Whilst I stayed with Nicholas, the mother and two children slept in the basement because it was considered unsuitable for a white man. I slept in the bed in one room and Nicholas slept on a cement floor in the other. The family were poor, lived in abominable conditions, but gave the best they had to this man from England.

God had used Nicholas to establish three churches, and it was an eye-opener to travel with him to see what was happening and to share. After spending a short period with him I asked if I might visit the couple whose name had been given to me by the missionaries I had met in England before leaving. The journey, I was told, would involve a taxi and a lorry ride.

We pushed our way into a Datsun 4-seater taxi, into which were crushed 8 people. As we drove along, I hung onto the door to prevent it falling off. We reached the lorry park and climbed aboard a lorry along with the now familiar goats and chickens.

Eventually we arrived at the home of David and Margaret

Mills. By Ghanaian standards the house was luxurious, certainly compared to what I had been living in the previous ten days, and what Nicholas Andoh had to endure. The Church of Pentecost had been very generous and built the house for the Mills family. Although we had never met before or had contact of any kind, David and I clicked immediately and over a short period of time became firm friends. I was treated like Father Christmas when I produced some small gifts. The enthusiastic response to the relatively insignificant presents I had brought left a lasting impression on me.

I had made a commitment to spend two weeks with Nicholas, and when David asked me to stay with them, I felt I should honour my word to Nicholas. I did, however, return to preach on a Tuesday evening, at the request of David Mills, at a church in Kwadaso, a suburb of Kumasi. My preaching must have been sufficiently good to impress David Mills, for he subsequently asked me if I would be willing to preach at McKeown Temple in Kumasi on the Easter Sunday.

I had no idea what the McKeown Temple was, its size or who McKeown was, the man after whom the Temple was named. By now I had been in Ghana for almost three weeks and agreed to extend the trip by one week in order to be able to carry out the preaching engagement.

In Genesis 42 we find Joseph Governor of all Egypt. Due to the famine in Canaan his brothers came down seeking food. In verse 6 we read *"so when Joseph's brothers arrived, they bowed down to him with their faces to the ground."* They did not recognise him, but he knew them, and in verse 9 it says that he then remembered his dreams about them. After so many years of waiting, trial, trouble and testing by the Lord, Joseph had come to the place where the dream could be fulfilled. Had it happened before, he might well have got conceited and lorded it over his brothers, but such was God's dealing with him that he had no desire to act in this way. In fact, the Bible account tells us that initially he pretended to be a stranger. His heart went out to them and so intense were the feelings he experienced that he had to turn away from them to conceal the fact that he was weeping.

God had dealt with Joseph in a remarkable way and even though he had brought him to a place of considerable authority in the land, the man's humility is more than evident.

I moved in with the Mills family for the week and on Easter Sunday was driven to the McKeown Temple. As it came in sight I was surprised by the size of the building. Long before we reached the entrance, we knew the service was underway because we could hear the joyful and enthusiastic singing. We went in through a side entrance, straight onto an elevated platform. The building was packed to the doors. Five thousand people were crammed into a space for about three thousand five hundred. From the moment we took our places on the platform, it was as if I was in a time warp. I had stepped into my dream. Everything I saw and experienced was an action replay of the vision I had received over 20 years previously in that small room in the Elim church in Dagenham. I knew what was going to happen next as the meeting progressed. I felt humbled, moved and overwhelmed by the goodness of God. I was grateful to God for making me wait so long, for there had been much in my life that needed to be dealt with by the loving hand of my Father.

Five thousand Ghanaians abandoned in worship is enough to reduce the stiffest upper lip of an Englishman to tears. I was no exception as I witnessed the enthusiasm, the total abandonment and commitment to God and the generosity of the people. They were incredible scenes, as all of the five thousand present took their turn to sing and dance their way to the front of the building to put their money in the offering. The bowl was over two feet in diameter and about eighteen inches deep, and was filled over and over again with notes. This alone took about one hour, and the whole time the congregation sang their songs of praise repeatedly.

As I got up to speak, it was exactly as I had seen it in the vision. The people responded and came forward as I gave the challenge. I was left in no doubt that God was fulfilling His word. The dream that had been in my heart for so long had become reality. On the one hand I was inspired that if God could do this, he could also accomplish the other things that he had spoken of concerning travelling, and reaching the world. I knew then I had the faith to see all those things happen because I had seen the Lord do it after having waited for over 20 years. But I was humbled as well, realising that God's timing is always perfect. I knew that had I got to Ghana earlier, I would have been intolerable to live with. God's man of faith and power for the hour would not have had many friends.

When I left Ghana, I came home with the utter conviction that dreams really do come true. On arrival in England, one of the first things I did was to buy items that I had noticed were needed in the Mills household and sent them out to them. Little did I realise this simple act of kindness would develop into something much more significant and that my dream would unfold in ways that even I had not anticipated. But it is a long way from Dagenham to Accra.

Chapter 2
A Mother's Dream

Mothers have high hopes for their sons. They want to see them grow up into men they can be proud of and often hold secret dreams in their hearts that they would love to see fulfilled. My mother was no exception. Two things in particular she felt God had spoken to her about were fulfilled, both of which were very significant.

I have often been reminded by Grace that when she first met me she thought I was the most big-headed person she had ever encountered. To her, it seemed as though this Norman Barnes fellow thought he knew everything, was always trying to take the role of leader in everything that happened, and was more than just secure in who he was. I admit freely there was more than an element of truth in what she felt.

At the age of 24 years she was worshipping at Bethel Pentecostal Church in Dagenham, but had heard that the Elim Church in the area was desperately in need of Sunday School teachers. Bethel had more than enough teachers, so Grace decided that there was no reason why she should not help with the other church. She informed the minister that she was leaving, who, quite understandably, failed to see things in quite the same light as Grace, but once her mind was made up she made tracks.

On the day that she entered the Elim Church, she was spotted by my mum, who decided that she was exactly the right girl for her Norman. How did she know when she had not even spoken to the girl? I can only assume that it must have been God speaking to her. This was the first dream that was placed in her heart, which she proceeded to pray about with considerable enthusiasm.

Within a short period of time Grace became involved with

the Good News team, which is where we first met. Embarrassed as I am to admit it, I had this habit at that time of kissing all the girls hallo and goodbye. Greeting them with a holy kiss, of course! Grace made it very plain through mutual friends that if I attempted to try this on her, I would receive a short, sharp, smack round the face! I got the message loud and clear!

Her negative feelings towards me did not stop a romance blossoming, and within six months of meeting we were engaged. I was only 18 years old at the time, and Grace, being a very proper lady, decided I would have to wait until I was 21 years old before we could get married, in 1964. My mum's first dream had been fulfilled.

We came home early from our honeymoon because we had run out of money. We literally had one halfpenny between us and when we returned to the furnished flat we had managed to acquire for rent, we had no food either. We lifted our hearts to God and decided to go and see my mum. We made no mention of the fact that we did not have any food, but because of a special offer at the supermarket, mum had obtained extra groceries. For no reason at all she offered them to us, which we accepted gratefully. That was the beginning of our walk of faith. For many years after that we would know what it was to have to pray in all our food. We learned to trust God in the small things first, and gradually found our faith increasing to believe for more. Eventually we would be able to impart faith to others and encourage them to believe the Lord for themselves.

Most married couples dream of owning a house, a place they can call their own. We were no different and made tentative enquiries about buying a house. We were eager to start a family, but children were not allowed in the furnished flat, so acquiring alternative accommodation became a matter of some urgency. My salary was not sufficient for a mortgage, however, and reluctantly we had to drop the idea of buying.

We heard about a flat available in another district for which 100 people had put their names down, and decided to add ours to the list. The list was reduced to two possibles, and we were still on it. We felt that God had given us the flat. We prayed, just in case we could be accused of presumption, "Lord, if it is not your will, we do not want the flat." We prayed it, but did not really mean it. We were completely on a high about what we felt was our impending move. Then we learned that the flat had gone to the other couple. We felt as if we had hit rock bottom.

I learned later that we were not the only ones who were disappointed. My mum shared our pain. As she looked at my sister, who seemed to be doing so well, buying her own house and generally prospering, she felt we were suffering an injustice. In desperation she prayed, "Lord, how is it that Ann, who is not really following you any more has everything, and Norman and Grace, who love and serve you have nothing. It can't be right!" As she waited on God, He gave her a vision of a building in which there was a main hall with a stage. The stage had blue curtains, and the hall had brown chairs. There was also a two-bedroomed flat attached to the building.

The vision was so vivid that the next time Grace and I visited her, the first thing she said to us was, "Norman, you are going to be a pastor." I became angry with her and told her what I felt about that in no uncertain terms. But my mum simply held the dream in her heart and prayed. Even though I told her adamantly "I don't want to be a pastor, I want to be an evangelist!," she just carried on believing what God had told her.

My idea of serving God was to be in the open air, preaching and seeing people come to the Lord, but my mum was convinced that the Lord had other ideas.

Six months later we were invited, along with my mum and dad, to preach at Chadwell Christian Mission in Goodmayes, Essex. As we walked into the building, mum

37

said, "this is the place I saw in the vision." To be absolutely sure she was right, she confirmed with the secretary of the Mission that a two bedroomed flat was attached to the building.

"You will be pastor of this place," she told me.

"I will not!" I replied angrily. "I've told you before, I do not want to be a pastor. I've got no time for it, and certainly not for this place. I don't want to care for all these old people. Anyway they haven't invited me."

"They will," was all she commented in that infuriatingly confident way that said quite clearly she knew better than her son about this one.

A short time after that preaching engagement I received a letter inviting me to be pastor of the Chadwell Christian Mission. It was totally ridiculous! I was only 24 years old and a dedicated Pentecostal, what on earth had possessed them to ask me to do the job! I was totally thrown, did not have the faintest idea what to do and eventually wrote back stating I would think and pray about it.

I was panicking. I only had six sermons, which I used on a rotational basis. The secret was, never to go to the same place to preach more than six times. If I became pastor of Chadwell Christian Mission, I would have to preach at least twice a week, which would mean one hundred sermons a year! There couldn't be that many in the Bible. I had to work so hard just to get one sermon together, I felt that I simply would not be able to keep going. I much preferred the "hit 'em and run" lifestyle I was leading, where, as far as I was concerned, six sermons covered all I wanted to say to people.

In this state of turmoil I attended a conference where a certain Edgar Trout was speaking. At the close of one of the meetings I joined a queue for prayer. As I reached the speaker, he said, "the Lord is calling you into something and you are worried about not having the word to speak. If you will wait on God and be faithful, He will give you his word." Encouraged by this, I took hold of the words he had spoken and believed them for all I was worth.

Responding hesitantly to the Mission's invitation, I was asked to go for a three week trial "to preach with a view". I knew that during that period I would be totally cleared out of all the ministry I had, and so decided to give them everything I'd got in the only way I knew how. Hopefully they would then change their minds about having me as pastor. I was as strong and firey, as black and white as I could be, and gave it to them between the eyes on prevailing prayer, healing, baptism in the Spirit, in fact all my favourite subjects.

The congregation actually only numbered about twelve, but there were others who had some kind of involvement which brought the total up to around twenty-five people. They suddenly appeared when it became known that a vote was to take place about my role as pastor.

So unhappy was I about the whole situation that I laid down further conditions before the Lord. "Thank you for your promise concerning supplying your word," I prayed, "but to be absolutely sure that this is what you want, I am going to put out a fleece. I want 100% support, a total vote in favour of Grace and I going to the Mission. If there is one no vote, or an abstention, I won't go." This was pushing things to the limit with the variety of people who were involved, but when the vote was taken up, we had 100% in favour.

My mum's second dream had been fulfilled. She was delighted, I was deflated. Eventually I got to the place where I could pray, "Lord, I'm not happy about it, but if this is where you want us, we will be obedient."

The World begins in Goodmayes

Abraham was a man who had a vision. The promise of God burned brightly in his heart and mind as he obeyed the Lord and left his country and people to go to a land that God would show him. He was going to be the father of a great nation, and he left all his familiar surroundings, the Bible tells us in Hebrews 11 v 8, even though he did not know where he was going. But it did not matter! His descendants were going to be as great in number as the stars in heaven, or the grains of sand on the seashore. He was totally confident of this fact and moved in faith, remaining sensitive to the voice of God.

When things do not work out as quickly as we would like, we start to doubt the vision we have been given and the dream begins to grow dim. Abraham was no exception. We read the following words in Genesis 15 v 1-3 *"after this, the word of the Lord came to Abraham in a vision: 'do not be afraid, Abraham. I am your shield, your very great reward'. But Abraham said, 'Oh sovereign Lord, what can you give me since I remain childless ... you have given me no children; so a servant in my house will be my heir.'".* Note the words, *"O sovereign Lord, what can you give me ...."* I wonder if Abraham sat in his tent at night thinking about the wonderful promise of God about a nation and a land to live in, then looking around him thought, "What on earth am I doing here?" It must have been very tempting to think he had got it all wrong and that he had deceived himself. The Lord had promised to make him a great nation, and here he was, in a tent, with not even one child to his name; and he was certainly not getting any younger.

I can identify with those feelings. God had given me a vision of the world, a tremendous vision of Africa, and here I was, in glorious Goodmayes, an area sandwiched between the two larger towns of Ilford and Romford, on the east side of London. I was the pastor of a Mission that was comprised almost totally of elderly people, and was actually being run down and phased out by its trustees. "What am I doing here?" I asked myself and the Lord on a number of occasions.

I may have been unhappy, but Grace was petrified. She

suddenly felt all the weight of responsibility of being a minister's wife descend on her. She now had to act according to her new status and learn how to look the part, even if she did not feel comfortable with it. She studied other ministers' wives carefully, noting how they managed to smile all the time in public and never seemed to raise their voices or lose their cool. This was not too easy for Grace, for she was always very down to earth and honest, saying what she felt whether it was acceptable or not. But she managed eventually to present the image she felt was expected of her, most of the time.

One of her first experiences at the Mission was to be invited to a women's 'World Day of Prayer' to hear a talk about prayer. It was a bitterly cold day, with snow on the ground. Grace dressed up for the weather in boots, scarf and winter coat. When she arrived for the start of the meeting, all the other women were there in their finest apparel, leaving Grace feeling very ashamed of her appearance.

At one point in the meeting they turned to her and asked her where she was from. She told them. "Oh, they have a new minister don't they?" they asked.

"Yes, that's right," said Grace, not giving anything away.

"Do you think you could ask the minister's wife if she would come and speak to this group?"

"Of course," she promised.

The minister's wife accepted the invitation, and on that occasion returned to speak dressed in all her finery.

There were very few opportunities for either of us to wear any finery in those early days. The building had to be rewired, redecorated, in fact completely overhauled and we worked at it day and night. I had given up my job to go self-employed as a builder and decorator, in order that I could give time to the church when it was necessary. I earned very little money and it was a real step of faith for both of us. We were totally thrust on God for our finances,

41

having just about enough money to pay the rent. Anything else we prayed for and saw God care for us in many wonderful ways.

Life would have been easier for us had we been able to move into the flat attached to the Mission, but unfortunately it was occupied and remained so for a year. This often meant a walk of several miles just to be at meetings, because we were unable to afford the money for public transport. My mum came with another word from the Lord for us, ''you will be in the flat in February,'' she prophesied. And indeed we were, but a year later than she expected.

''You got the month right mum.'' I told her, ''you were just a bit out on the year.''

Mum, however, saw the wisdom of God in the delay. ''If you had moved straight into the flat when you became pastor of the Mission,'' she said, ''because of your need for accommodation and your desire to move out of the furnished flat, your priority would have been your home. But now you have had to wait a year, and give yourselves totally to the work, your priority is the people.''

Never a truer word was spoken. Most of the folk involved at the beginning were elderly, and in spite of what I had said about them in my fit of pique with my mum, Grace and I learned to care for them. We often sat with them overnight when they were dying, watched them die and then laid them out. So good, in fact, were we at the job, that the local undertaker offered us the chance of work if we ever needed another job! It was a traumatic time for us, but through sitting with the dying we learnt a lot about God, the reality of the Gospel in people's lives and the peace of the Lord.

The Mission became, in fact, something of a centre for funerals for a while. Not only did we bury folk from our own congregation, but many people in the area had some sort of connection with the Mission, and it became the natural place for them to have their funeral ceremonies. I conducted an endless number of them, not entirely without their lighter moments.

I was, if nothing else, a quick learner. I soon mastered the accepted procedures for conducting funerals and knew that at the beginning of the service the minister was supposed to walk in front of the coffin, reading the scriptures as it came into the church.

On one occasion the funeral director and coffin bearers gathered at the door, ready to carry in the coffin. I waited for the signal from the director. When it came, I proceeded down the aisle, reading the appropriate passage. As I got half way to the front of the church, an awful feeling began to grip me. Without looking round, I had this sense that no-one was following me. As inconspicuously as possible, I glanced behind me. My feelings of dread were confirmed. I was alone. I could almost feel the blood drain from my face. Something had gone wrong; why were they not following me? I could not go back to the coffin and start again! What was I to do? I felt as if every eye was on me. I was still walking slowly and reading, panic beginning to seize my mind. In the end, I did the only thing I could have done. I decided to brave it out and carry on as if nothing was wrong. As I got to the front and turned round I hoped that no one would notice my discomfort. I nodded to the undertaker to come to the front and continued to read the scriptures while they walked down the aisle. I had never felt so relieved to see a coffin as when that one finally reached the front of the church.

Getting coffins into church, however, was not the only cause of problem. I felt especially nervous at the first funeral I conducted in a crematorium. It is normal practice on these occasions for the minister to press a button to make the coffin disappear at a certain point in the service. On this occasion an official seated at the back of the building had to carry out this small, but important task. Because of my nervousness, I must have read the scriptures in an uncharacteristically quiet fashion. The signal for the official to press the button was the familiar part of the passage that reads "ashes to ashes, dust to dust". As I got to the end of the reading, I looked up to see the coffin still visible and not moving to where it should have gone. In a state of alarm, my eyes went immediately to the back of the building, to see the man in charge of the button falling asleep. I felt sick in the pit of my stomach, my mind was racing, trying to find a solution to the situation.

To everyone's amazement, I started to read the whole passage of scripture again. I got to the key part a second time and still the coffin did not move. By this time, people were looking at each other, obviously feeling embarrassed. But not as embarrassed as I! In desperation, as I got to the end of the reading for a second time, I said a very loud 'Amen.' At that the official sat bolt upright in his seat, realised what had happened and pressed the button.

Caring for people took its toll. Another occasion for a night watch came when one of the members became ill. We sat up all night and when morning came, I went to work. This vigil lasted for three days and nights, during which I had no sleep. It dawned on me that I might be overdoing it when, one day when I was working on a roof, I found myself dropping off to sleep, fortunately not dropping off the roof.

At the end of four sleepless nights and days, I came home from work, got to the front door and waited for Grace to answer the doorbell. As she opened the door, I simply pitched forward and fell headlong into the hallway. Somehow she managed to drag me to bed where I crashed out asleep. For twenty-four hours I slept without a murmur; in fact Grace even wondered momentarily if I'd died. When I woke up, I had something to eat and then slept solid for another twenty-four hours. I was totally exhausted and I am convinced it was only the long period of sleep that saved me from some kind of breakdown.

Unfortunately this incident was not an isolated case. I

collapsed in similar fashion another three times as a result of overdoing things. It was at moments like these I would ask myself again why I was flogging myself at the Mission when God had so clearly shown me that I was somehow going to be involved in a ministry that would touch different parts of the world. My patience was sorely tried.

The Mission were naturally concerned about me collapsing in this fashion and offered to support me part-time financially. Then I collapsed again from overwork, and it was decided that I needed to be able to give myself to the work of the church fulltime. I was supported to the tune of £10 per week, although I was asked if I could live on less by some members.

We still found it necessary to pray for all of our food, clothing and other necessities of life. We only had one carpet in the whole flat, which we carried with us from room to room, and when we had guest speakers, they stayed in the first room we were able to decorate, with the only carpet.

One of the speakers who gave time to us at the Mission was Cecil Cousens, who brought a ministry of faith, and moved prophetically to bless people. He became a father figure to me in many ways and spoke at the meeting where Grace and I officially went fulltime to serve the church. He was responsible for causing a definite turning point in our lives. He was aware of our desire to serve God and the dreams I held in my heart and on one visit prophesied to both Grace and myself. To Grace he said that she would no longer be a Martha, but a Mary who would sit at the feet of Jesus. This spoke to her deeply about the need she had to always be busy and doing things. To me he prophesied that God would change me from a lion to a lamb. This challenged me about my dealings with people and also had a great effect on the impatience that welled up periodically. I became much more at rest that God would work things out in His own time and I was to get on with the job to hand.

A young girl by the name of Christine was a regular

teacher in the Sunday School. When Grace first saw her, she did not ask "who is that?" but "what is that?" Chris had bleached, blonde hair, had plucked all her eyebrows and wore very heavy make-up. But she did come regularly to teach and attend the Sunday services. While the six day war was taking place in Israel, I preached about the second coming of Christ and as a result of that message, she gave her life to Christ.

Her fiancé, a young man called John Norton, was not too thrilled by her conversion. When they went to the pub with their friends, Chris would sit outside in the car, refusing to go in. This only served to make John angrier with her and very much against the Mission. At that time she, and we, were convinced she was doing the right thing, 'making a stand' as we called it.

John did come occasionally to meetings, however, but it was not unusual for him to storm out before the end. He could not cope with all that he saw and heard, but in spite of that began to read the New Testament. He came to one particular meeting where a certain Arthur Campbell was preaching. When an appeal was given for people to accept Jesus as Lord of their lives, John responded.

He and Chris not only became our very close and firm friends, but also very influential in the life of the Mission, until some years later they would take on pastoral responsibility for the church.

As Grace and I settled more and more into life at the Mission, so a new dream began to be born in our hearts; to see a live, thriving church develop that would be a practical demonstration of the life and power of Christ. There was certainly never a lack of anything to do. On Sundays, the day would start with a prayer meeting, followed by the morning meeting. People fasted all day every Sunday, so there would be a lunch time prayer meeting, then Sunday School, a further prayer meeting before the open air witness, followed closely by the evening meeting. To round off the day nicely there would be an after church rally.

As we put out the chairs for each meeting, we made a point of praying over each one, crying to God to fill them, and fulfil the burdens and vision He had placed in our hearts. Our prayers were not answered immediately and because a good number of the chairs were empty, I would remove the last six rows before the meeting began. When I came out to start the service, people had put them back.

I must admit that in the early days, the meetings were not without difficulties. There always seemed to be arguments about who would sit where; often when I preached I would have one old man who was deaf banging his stick on the floor shouting "you don't have to shout," while others were crying out at the same time, "speak up, we can't hear you."

Nevertheless, the size of the congregation slowly began to grow. Friends came and people began to be saved. We circularised the area of six thousand people twice with literature and preached on every street corner. We prayed and fasted as a people for the whole of Easter each year. Everyone would arrive at 9.30 a.m. in the morning and pray until 5.00 p.m. in the evening. God visited us in remarkable ways, reminiscent of the prayer meetings we had as a youth group in the Elim Church in Dagenham. Sometimes the Holy Spirit would sweep into the room and we would all be prostrate on the floor before the Lord. A number of men who are now fulltime ministers still remember those prayer meetings and much of what is evident today in the life of the Mission, is a result of what we prayed then. The key to everything was prayer. All that we did was soaked in prayer.

Today, the fellowship has a prayer team that is dedicated to praying through many of the issues, projects and problems that we are all concerned with. Grace often makes the point that capital does not last for ever. We cannot live on the prayers of yesterday.

Although the Lord had clearly spoken to me about not

seeing a miracle ministry personally for some time as far as healing was concerned, this did not prevent us, as a body of God's people, praying for and expecting Him to heal the sick. Miracles did take place. We prophesied over three women who were unable to have children, and later all three conceived. We prayed for John Norton who like me, had suffered from short-sightedness and the Lord healed his eyes. We prayed for many women with gynaecological problems who were healed and never had to go into hospital.

One noteable case of healing was a man called Francis, who had to wear a steel corset because of spinal problems. He came to the Mission, gave his life to Christ, and was healed at the same time. He took off the steel corset, never to wear it again.

God, it seems, is also interested in preventative medicine. One day while Grace was praying, He spoke to her about one of the young women in the church who was three months pregnant. Grace was, to say the least, somewhat taken aback when the Holy Spirit seemed to be saying the baby the woman, called Sue, was carrying would die. She was in fact greatly distressed by this revelation as the information began to sink in, and she was sure that she was not merely hearing the product of a vivid imagination.

"What do I do about this word?" she asked me.

"I don't just think God tells you a baby is going to die for no reason," I ventured. "There is absolutely no profit in us having such knowledge for six months, then when the baby dies, say 'the Lord told us'. Nor do I think there is any profit in being able to go to the parents and say, 'well, actually, your baby is going to die'. God is not that kind of God. The only reason he can have told us is so that we can pray it will not happen."

We determined to fast and pray for one day a week, binding the powers of darkness that were seeking to take the life of the child, and praying that God would perform whatever miracle was necessary.

48

Eight months into the pregnancy Sue went into hospital and gave birth to the baby prematurely. Grace and I were on tenterhooks, waiting to hear some news. At last the 'phone rang. An excited father told me, "I've got a little girl, she's 4lbs and is in intensive care in an incubator." As much as I tried to sound it I was not in the least bit excited. The more I heard, the more downhearted I became. It sounded grim. After I had relayed the news to Grace, all we could do was to pray.

"Lord, what are you doing?" we asked in desperation. "You haven't taken us this far to mock us."

Within twenty-four hours the baby began to improve, came out of intensive care, and in a short space of time started to put on weight. Sue asked the staff why the baby had been born prematurely.

"The baby was born one month early" they said, "with the umbilical cord wrapped around her neck four times. If your pregnancy had gone the full nine months, your little girl would have been so big, the cord would have strangled her and she would have been dead at birth."

God had saved the life of the baby by allowing her to be born one month early. When she was born, the cord slipped off her neck easily and she was perfectly healthy.

We are grateful to God for all these healings and many more that we have been privileged to see since taking responsibility for the work of the Mission, not least in our own lives. We will not be content, however, until we see the Lord attesting His word in signs and wonders, miracles and healings, and a clear demonstration of His mighty power. Nothing less will satisfy us, and we are convinced that we will see it in the not too distant future.

Split the Difference

One thing I have always appreciated about the Bible is the absolute honesty of all the writers. This may seem a strange thing to say about the book that Christians world-wide hold dear and regard as being the inspired words of God. But it is not just that it reveals the truth in the positive sense. The writers were not afraid to report the less savoury moments of life. We are given fairly detailed and frank accounts about biblical heroes' lives, and their weaknesses, failures and sin are not covered up.

Take, for example, Paul and Barnabas. Paul was a small man by all accounts, but one of the giants of New Testament history. A man who was given incredible revelation by the Holy Spirit, fiery evangelist, a man of considerable knowledge and someone to whom most of us look for example and inspiration. Barnabas, son of encouragement, a man who clearly had a caring heart and in many ways must have been the ideal travelling partner for Paul. Two men of God, with the call of the Lord on their lives who experienced the joy of seeing many turn to Christ and churches all over the known world being established. But they nearly came to blows!

The story is well known. Barnabas wanted to take John Mark with them on their journeying further, Paul did not. An argument developed between them, and so fierce was their disagreement, that they had to part company. It was a sad moment, almost certainly an avoidable one, but neither man would back down and the result was a split in the partnership.

I am so glad that incidents like these are recorded for us. Not because I enjoy seeing people fail and make mistakes, but it does remind us we are all human and prone to failure and weakness.

It would be dishonest of me, if I did not recount the fact that my dreams suffered setbacks and severe batterings at times. As I got increasingly involved in the activities of the Mission, so my vision enlarged to see a fellowship of people grow that would be a positive demonstration of the love and power of God, and a light in the darkness, and was expending considerable energy in seeing that goal achieved.

I was travelling with my long time friend John Noble on one occasion in his car. During the course of the conversation, he mentioned how he had been reading Watchman Nee's book about church life and had received a revelation about meeting in homes. As he continued to share what he felt God was saying to him, I began to see something of what he was talking about and found myself warming to the idea. In fact, in my usual fashion, I got very enthusiastic about it. I had not yet realised the full implications of what John was saying.

He was, quite naturally, intent on seeing his revelation worked out practically, and in order to do that, felt he had to take certain steps that would lead him away from any further involvement with the Mission. Up to that time he had supported us as much as he was able in between fulfilling his own ministry commitments. Several young people for whom I felt a strong affection, decided they wanted to be involved with John in this new thing he was doing, and started to meet with him.

I got desperately hurt in all these developments. I am not saying that John was necessarily to blame, but I could not understand why these young people were going with him, or why John could not just simply throw in his lot with the Mission and bring them with him.

Not long after this incident, the whole issue of law and grace became a hot potato, almost too hot for many people to handle. To the evangelical world at the time, the house churches seemed to be getting into license and virtually allowing anything to happen. All kinds of stories circulated and any number of accusations were made. To the house churches, much of the evangelical way of thinking was legalistic, had nothing to do with the grace of God and was basically a system of man-made rules and regulations. I freely confess now that I, and consequently the Mission, were very legalistic. As I looked at John Noble and all that he was doing I saw, for example, that the house churches seemed to be free to do anything they chose on a Sunday, where I did not feel free to do anything except attend meetings of one kind or another. Although I tried to push down my hurt, it continually resurfaced in a form of anger and I became the arch opponent of the house church movement, ably supported by Grace. I did not waste any opportunity I was given to preach against it, and continued in this vein for several years.

After a number of years of separation and antagonism on my part, I started to build bridges towards those who had been my friends in the house churches. I began to spend regular time, once a month, with John Noble and Maurice Smith, where I was able to share my heartaches and hurts and clear up misunderstandings. It was a slow process, but healing of emotional wounds often is.

Grace was still an arch opponent and refused flatly to have anything to do with house churches. When I went to their Sunday evening meetings after we had finished our own at the Mission, she would let me go alone. I enjoyed the lively, informal gathering so much, that occasionally I would take John and Chris Norton with me, but Grace's only comment was, "you are going into error. You will take me into hell." Her reaction, however, was more out of fear that I would be hurt again, rather than anything else, and she was determined not to let that happen again.

The bond between John Noble and myself grew stronger and stronger, and our original friendship was renewed. The reconciliation was made complete when we 'made covenant' with one another. We agreed to work and walk together, and stick with each other whatever happened. Slowly but surely the Mission found its way into the house church movement. Grace came in much more slowly than I, as all her own hurts were healed. John Noble kept reaching out to her, and eventually her heart was won.

During this period of transition, it seemed at times that we were in a no win situation. We received criticism from all sides. From the evangelicals because we were associating with the house churches, and from the house churches because we were still meeting in a building. The fledgling movement had not yet realised that its membership would one day outgrow even the largest front room. Now, many are buying their own buildings.

With the reconciliation that took place between John Noble and myself, came a new impetus as far as pursuing my dream of seeing an effective fellowship develop and grow. My vision was widened as a result of becoming involved with the house churches, with their emphasis on caring relationships, the oneness of the Body of Christ, and the vital part that each member of that Body had to play. But this vision was to receive a severe battering.

We entered a period that was marked by a new emphasis coming to the fore. Many were reading Juan Carlos Ortiz's book 'Call to Discipleship' and trying to apply the truths contained in it. The issues of authority, submission and discipleship were the focus of much attention, and the Mission was no exception in its attempts to embody these aspects of the Christian's walk into the life of the Church. This meant that we touched areas of each other's lives that would not normally have ever been thought about had we continued in our very heavy programme of meetings, but not much more in the way of fellowship and involvement with each other.

One morning I received a 'phone call from one of the leading figures in the Mission, asking me to meet him at his house. Sensing that this was going to be more than a social visit, I asked John Norton to accompany me. When we arrived, there were three men waiting to see us: the Sunday School Superintendent, the Secretary and the Treasurer.

"You've asked me to come here so you can tell me what you want", was my opening line. I was annoyed that there were three men present, and I had not been told.

"No" they replied, "we want to ask questions".

"That is not true", I insisted.

With that they began to make all kinds of accusations. "The presence of God is not in the meetings" they asserted. The fact that people were being saved and healed seemed to be totally ignored.

"Well, that is not all my responsibility" I replied in my defence. "I cannot just clap my hands and bring about the presence of God that you say is lacking".

The argument continued, and finally the three men stated that they wanted to go to the whole church with the matter. I felt totally churned up. I could sense something about to happen, that everything inside me fought against. I had worked so hard for so many years and now everything was being threatened. I agreed to do as they wished, but made it clear that if a vote was taken up over the issue, and it went against me, I would resign. If it went against them, however, I would expect them to repent or leave.

The church was called together and the matter laid clearly before them. The vote was taken up and the majority voted in my favour. Fifteen people left altogether as a result of the incident, including the three men and a couple of deacons, but victorious was the last thing that I felt. For the next few days we struggled to find some emotional stability, aware that something akin to a limb being wrenched out of a body had taken place. The fellowship was still small enough to feel the loss of fifteen people with considerable pain. It was as though a gaping hole had been blown in the life of the group and we needed time to adjust and collect ourselves.

A split in a church, however big or small, is never pleasant, but one good thing came out of the incident immediately. A young man called Norman Cook said, "if that is the truth in the Church, I want to know more," and as a result was soundly converted.

This traumatic time also taught us to look carefully at what we had produced in terms of fellowship and it was only later, with hindsight, that we recognised the faulty foundations that we had put into the general life of the Church. We determined from that moment not to compromise on honesty and integrity. We did not allow any gossip, and confronted anyone who carried on in this way. We decided to confront every problematic issue full in the face, no matter how painful.

We became convinced of the need, as far as church growth was concerned, to major on quality rather than quantity. Because of this policy, people who came to the Mission more than once from another church in the area were told, "your minister will be receiving a 'phone call from us to ask if he knows you are at our meetings." This usually kept people from hopping from one church to another, but even those who persisted in coming to the Mission, found the way in difficult. It was deliberately made so, in order that the person concerned, and the Mission leadership, could be sure of their motives and the rightness of the move.

It took some time to recover from the loss of so many members, both in terms of the life of the Church and the emotional upheaval that it caused for many of us. Our dream had certainly received a severe battering, but Jesus has a way of taking shattered dreams and putting them back together again. God can take the worst moments of our life and somehow bring good out of them, and we were to discover this as the years following showed increased growth, especially of young people being added to the church.

One of the most exciting moments in the life of the Mission for Grace and myself, was to see the fulfilment of words we had spoken many years before. "We want to do ourselves out of a job," we had both determined, and the moment finally arrived when we are able to hand over the day to day running of the Mission to the first converts, John and Chris Norton. By this time I had been to Ghana and finding more doors opening for ministry in this country and abroad. This meant increasing time away from home and consequently less time to spend with the people who had become very much a family to me at the Mission.

It took longer than I would have liked to arrive at the position where we could hand over responsibility to someone else, mostly because God had to deal with insecurities, needs and pride in my own life. It was not an easy step to make, but we have never regretted making it, and are thrilled with all that John, Chris and the other leaders are doing in serving our burden and vision for the work of God. It has released us to wider spheres of ministry and played a very large part in enabling my dream of reaching the world to find expression. Now we have complete freedom to travel to and through other continents without having to worry about what is happening back at home.

We are thrilled to see the work of the Mission continue to thrive, recently changing its name to Chadwell Christian Fellowship. Not only has the congregation continued to grow, with new converts being added to its numbers very regularly, but it also runs its own primary school, and has joined forces with another fellowship to run a secondary school.

The Trustees of the Mission, the Shaftesbury Society, were dubious about my appointment at the beginning, but have come to appreciate what God has done and have been firmly behind us for many years. They recently funded another of our dreams, the building of a block of flats beside the church building, designed for elderly, single and disabled people.

It is so thrilling being a dreamer. Once a particular dream has been fulfilled, you find another taking its place. God has put a vision in my heart to plant out churches in other areas and see men and women from our fellowship moving into those areas and taking responsibility for the work. In feptember 1987 we had already begun this and it is planned that twenty-five people will actually move out to another area close by to establish a new fellowship. Of one thing, however, I am also certain, our policy of never getting people involved at all costs will remain for any new work that is begun. We will always go for quality rather than quantity, which I trust will remain a hallmark of all we do, whether at home, in other parts of this country, or in our involvement with other countries around the world.

Chapter 3
Developing Links

My first trip to Ghana in 1979 was the fulfilment of a dream that I had held in my heart for over twenty years, but would prove to be far more influential in my life than I could ever have imagined.

Many times in our lives God shows us steps that He wants us to take, and it is only later when we look back on a certain period of time, we can see that those small steps were but the beginning of something far greater. They are often the keys to unlocking far more opportunities and a wider field of service than we could ever have conceived. So it was for me and my visit to Ghana.

In many ways I was thrilled and thankful to the Lord for being able to see my dream come true and would have been happy to leave it there, but the trip left a lasting impression on me. All that I had ever heard about Third World poverty and need, I had experienced first hand. It helped to put the world in proper perspective, for I realised that two-thirds of the people on this planet lived as the Ghanaians did, with a desperate lack of the basics of life such as sanitation, medical care, education, transportation, and the most rudimentary forms of technology.

Grace and I had always had an interest in world mission, and this is reflected in the life of the Mission, where an overseas vision was always nurtured and maintained. Missionaries on furlough were often invited to speak, and the Mission supported and cared for them.

In spite of all I knew and had heard of missionary work, I was still unprepared for the ecstatic reaction from the Mills family in Kwadaso when I gave them, what seemed to me, quite insignificant gifts. When I handed over the tea, coffee, sugar, sweets, soap, toothpaste etc, the missionary family treated me as if I'd given them presents of infinite value.

Through talking to and getting to know David Mills, I became aware of the low expectations that he and many other missionaries had as far as ongoing support from the West was concerned. By spending time with the family, I became aware of the things that they were lacking, simple items such as pads of paper, pens, dried milk and many basic food stuffs. I began to make notes every time they mentioned that they were short of something, although they were not aware of what I was doing.

The more time I spent with the Mills family, the longer the list of items became. While driving with David in his car, it would be obvious something was wrong mechanically. When I enquired about this, David would reply that it took at least six months to get hold of spare parts for cars.

I was determined to do something about this situation. When I got back to England, I contacted all the relevant car dealers, got the spare parts that David needed for his car, and within six weeks they were in his hands.

I also sent out food parcels containing items that were virtually unobtainable in Ghana, and after receiving very warm letters of thanks in return, began to realise that there was a way in which we could actually help and care for people overseas. By this time I was also beginning to share what I had experienced in Africa with various churches who invited me to speak. The reactions in each congregation were always a mixture of astonishment at the conditions I described, under which the majority of Ghanaian people were living, excitement at what God was evidently doing in great power in terms of phenomenal growth, and challenge that Christians in much more affluent countries seemed to have so much in terms of resources of people and money, but were unable to make the same effect for the Gospel's sake on the world around them.

As a result of these visits to churches and fellowships in different parts of the country, I began to receive money for the work we were trying to do for our friends in Ghana. It soon became necessary to consider forming a separate agency to deal with the money and gifts that were being channelled our way. Peter Martin, the Mission's administrator, my close friend and right-hand man, suggested we should call what we were doing Links International, since this seemed to convey very clearly what we were attempting to do.

So Links International was born, not with a fanfare of trumpets, but in a small side street in Goodmayes, Essex. We had a deep desire to serve the Church and bless people in whatever way we could. Time and time again we were amazed that what we did seemed so little, yet brought such tremendous blessing to people.

The contact with Ghana grew ever stronger, with Grace and myself, plus others, returning to visit almost every year from 1981 onwards. On almost every occasion we were conscious of some need that local Christians or community were unable to meet.

The school of 600 pupils in Koforidua was one of two run by the Church of Pentecost. The educational equipment and teaching aids in use in the schools made the so called lack in British schools look like positive abundance. Each class had one book for each subject which the teacher held and the only supply of children's reading books were located in the headmistress' room. There was a chronic shortage for everybody at every age group. The books they did possess were hopelessly out of date and extremely worn.

We felt constrained to do something about this and returned to England determined to find a way of helping. We raised enough money to buy items of equipment and were thrilled to be able to send out reading aids, pens, pencils, rulers, in fact everything the children would need to assist their education.

We could keep on sending out books, but the needs in the country are so great, we continually consult with leaders in the Church to decide the best use for the sterling we have available for their use.

I stood in a meeting one evening in a small village that had never before had a European stay overnight. My two friends, John Noble and Dave Bilbrough were accompanying me on this particular trip. I was in the full flow of my ministry, the electricity was cut off and everything went pitch black. In that situation dark is dark. It is almost impossible to see anything. I waited while around me there was obvious movement and suddenly a small light glowed. The wick of an oil lamp was touched by the flame and once again we had sufficient light.

The lamp was held near me so I could read the Bible, which was fine for everyone else. Within a matter of seconds, almost every insect in the neighbourhood made a beeline for the lamp. Flying ants, mosquitoes, flies and moths all decided that the lamp looked very inviting and I spent the rest of the time fighting with them, whilst trying to minister earnestly from the word of God.

It has been known, on such occasions, for the dry palm leaves that act as a canopy, to actually catch fire as a result of the use of these lamps, and a fire fighting operation is carried out before the meeting can continue. "This happens regularly" someone told me. "What we really need is a generator". I made a note of this but said nothing.

The same village embarrassed us with its generosity. Most of the people lived in dire poverty, yet they fed us until we could eat no more. They loaded up our vehicle with fruit and vegetables, and then gave us presents and money. We were overwhelmed, but knew it was no use refusing, for they would simply feel they had not given enough and try to find more to give us.

When we returned to England, I knew what I wanted to do. By making people aware of the need we were able to send out not one, but two generators, one for the village and the other for the Bible School, which was experiencing considerable problems whenever the power was cut.

We received a request from the Church of Pentecost, asking if we would be willing to invest in a printing machine for them. They already had one machine which was working flat out, and was basically inadequate for all they were producing. We gladly took this on board and it was not too long before we were able to ship out the machine they wanted. But even this is not fulfilling all their needs in terms of the printed matter that they are producing. When you are dealing with a Church of a quarter of a million people that is growing at the rate of one new church every two days, it becomes quite a task to supply all the necessary literature.

On one occasion we made an appeal in Britain for clothing for the Ghanaians. Within a short period of time we were inundated with clothing, a lot of which had to be dumped because, to be quite honest, it was rubbish and totally worn out. It would have been an insult to send some of it, especially when we considered how generous the Africans had been to us. There was no consideration given as to the needs of the people in such a hot climate. What was left was still a sizeable amount, however, which was parcelled up and sent as a gift to the Church.

About the same time the government in Ghana had been pressurizing the Church of Pentecost to be relevant to the needs of the poor. They had been told that if they were going to continue to be a positive force, they would have to affect the less fortunate in society.

The Church had already learnt from its mistakes in the country of Togo. They had overseas missionaries working with Ghanaians in a clinic, which was very successful. The missionaries felt they knew better than the Ghanaians, and against all advice, closed the clinic and started children's work. Shortly afterwards there was a change of government and because of the lack of social involvement by the Church of Pentecost, all its assemblies were officially closed down and went underground. Had they kept the clinic going, they would have been able to maintain their witness. Thankfully the situation has improved again in recent years.

The Church of Pentecost was not about to let the same thing happen in Ghana. They decided, therefore, to give most of the clothes we sent to them to the poor and needy. They knew about two leper colonies and gave the clothing to them. As a result, they received T.V. and radio coverage and the work was given a very high profile.

We have also raised £12,000 to buy a coach for the Church, sent out barrel loads of medical equipment, spare parts for all sorts of motorised vehicles, and during the famine that the world's press almost totally missed, or ignored, two tons of food.

Perhaps the most valuable way Links has been able to help, has been through the sending out of man-power to assist in various areas of work. I was approached by a young doctor called Graham Deakin from Bristol, who had just finished his medical training. Before he began practising as a G.P. he wanted to get some Third World experience. He felt that a private practice would be very middle-class, and he really wanted to see and experience how the rest of the world lived. Could I help? Of course I could, and within a very short space of time, Graham, his wife Ruth and their two children were off to Dunkwa in Ghana for nine months to work in a medical unit. Needless to say, Graham received all the experience, and more, that he desired.

The problem of getting spare parts for vehicles and then the length of time it actually took to get them repaired, began to impress itself on me more and more. I began to see a need for the Church of Pentecost to train its own mechanics and set up its own workshop, thereby giving people employment and saving considerable sums of money. In order to do that, however, there would need to be someone capable, not only of repairing vehicles, but also of making spare parts if the need arose.

I returned to England after one trip with this idea buzzing

around my head, and, before long I had thought of exactly the right man. After a lot of discussion and planning, Malcolm Cummins with his wife Barbara and their two sons, left for Accra, the capital of Ghana in 1986, supported by their home fellowship in Collier Row, Romford. Their mandate was to set up a vehicle repair workshop and train mechanics to do the work.

Malcolm made a considerable impact on the scene, saving the Church of Pentecost thousands of pounds with his business acumen and his willingness to confront unscrupulous suppliers about their prices.

It has not all been one-way traffic, however. Links also raised money to bring people from Ghana to England. A number of the leading pastors have visited the United Kingdom and have been a blessing to many Christians with their ministry and stories of all that God is doing in their own country.

Joshua was also another Links project. He was financed to come to England and learn the print trade at the London School of Printing, with all his living expenses and the course paid for.

How God has taken such a small operation as Links International and used it, never ceases to amaze me. Never in my wildest imaginations could I have foreseen how a dream to go to Africa would develop into such an ongoing involvement.

What I saw an an incredible adventure, I now realise was only a doorway into something far greater. Even though I would have been forever grateful to God for seeing that one dream fulfilled, I am nevertheless excited to see the work expanding and now have so many projects to consider, it is mainly a case of sorting out priorities in deciding which one we will tackle next.

In our contact with various missionaries around the world, we became aware of a very important factor in their lives. They quickly lost touch with what was happening in their homeland as far as the Christian scene was concerned. When they returned on furlough after three years on the mission field, they were often hopelessly out of date with current teaching, ministry and songs. When they attended meetings, they did not understand all the current in-house references, were not able to join in with the new songs of worship and had great difficulty in reorientating themselves.

In order to help them overcome these difficulties, we began to send ministry and worship tapes to them. The missionaries we knew were the sort of people who never had any time to listen to tapes when they were at home, but out on the field they received these cassettes with eagerness. People like Shirley Chapman, a bible translator with the Wycliffe Bible Translators in Brazil, and Ian Farr in India, were thrilled by the regular input these tapes provided. It was not unusual to hear that they had been played so much, they were literally worn out.

This small part of our ministry is developing. David Mills, now leading a work in England, is preparing a whole series of teaching tapes for African leaders. This will provide pastors with a whole set of ministry cassettes, along with the recorders if they are needed.

On a trip to India, I met a German by the name of Jochen Tewes. He was responsible for running a very large orphanage. I was moved by the needs of this work and subsequently arranged for various items to be sent out. The orphanage also had a printing activity that was running less than efficiently. In our own fellowship we had a printer who could sort out the mess and get the whole organisation running well. I approached Ernie Peters, who with his wife Olive, agreed to go to India for six months.

There are two remarkable things about this little episode. It was not just that Ernie and Olive did all that was asked of them, and more, but the fact that they were both over sixty years of age grew to be a real challenge to many younger men and women, who up to that time had never considered serving God in another country, even for a short period of time.

The second noteworthy point is that as a young woman, wishing to embark on a career in nursing, Olive felt called to the mission field and dreamed of going to India. Ernie, her fiancé at the time, told her quite clearly, "I don't feel called to India, but I do feel that we should be married, so I'm afraid you will have to forget the mission field."

Olive agreed to the marriage, but hid the dream of India in her heart. When we asked them to go to work at the orphanage for six months, the feeling that she had experienced as a young woman resurfaced and an incredibly happy Olive was able to testify to a dream fulfilled forty years later.

Such is the God we serve. How distorted our view of Him is at times. I am sure that many people would have condemned Olive for not going to the mission field, accusing her of being disobedient, putting marriage before the work of God. The Lord, however, sees the heart and knows our deepest desires. He longs to see our dreams fulfilled as much as we do and will work with us, sometimes inpite of us, to bring about the purposes he has for our lives.

We feel privileged that Links International is not only the outworking of a vision God gave to us, but it is also being instrumental in helping to fulfil other people's dreams. The one thing we have always been clear about, however, is that it is not another missionary society. People are never sent out to serve in other countries unless they are supported financially by another body, for example, their local church. Graham and Ruth Deakin were cared for excellently by the Bristol Christian Fellowship whilst they were in Ghana, and Malcolm and Barbara Cummins were looked after in much the same way by their own fellowship, Collier Row, Romford. In this way it becomes the fellowship's responsibility to send people out. Links International is happy to provide fares, expenses and other capital expenditure, but the salaries are found by the church.

Our vision to reach the world and the opportunities that exist, are being presented to a large section of the house church movement through Links and other agencies such as Supplyline. We are encouraged, however, by the strong links that are being forged with the Evangelical Missionary Alliance; Worldwide Evangelisation Crusade; The Dirty Hands Project and Derek Prince Ministries, to name but a few.

Every time we visit Ghana we become aware of more projects that we can get involved with. No matter how much we give, I never ceased to be amazed by the Ghanaian Christians that we meet and have the privilege of ministering to. I was talking to one of the pastors on our last visit in 1987.

"I have a problem" he confided in me.

"What is that?" I asked.

"Well, in the district I am responsible for there are twelve villages. I have now planted a church in every village. I have nowhere else to go. What can I do?"

"That sounds like a blessing to me, not a problem" I replied, wishing we could experience the same sort of problem here in England.

This man's story is repeated over and over again in Ghana. The Church is growing at the rate of two new churches every three days, and in Ghana these centres are not called churches until they have fifty members. In spite of all that God has done, I realise that we have only just begun when it comes to seeing dreams fulfilled. Men and women of vision in Ghana, in spite of all their lack of facilities and material goods, are reaping a mighty harvest. At a convention we attended, 153 people were saved in four days, and statistics show that once they have been baptised, almost all converts remain true to the Lord.

Their zeal for evangelism, their faithfulness in commitment to prayer, their abandonment to worship, their sheer enthusiasm and exuberance about the things of God, and their sacrificial giving, from a people who do not know where the next day's food is coming from, leaves me in no doubt that it is impossible for us to outgive and outserve our Ghanaian brothers and sisters. We have much to learn from them and may God save us from ever believing that we have it all to give to them.

Links International, under God's hand, is growing and becoming a creditable overseas service, reaching out wherever it can to serve and care. Our dream is to inspire people to give, to pray and to go. We are constantly finding new situations to be involved with and are thrilled by the challenges and opportunities. Links is a vital part of a fulfilment of the vision God placed in my heart many years previously and I can only humbly acknowledge, ''God has done this, and it is marvellous in our eyes.''

Chapter 4
More than one way to have Children

"It is very unlikely that you will ever be able to have children." The words hit us like the shock waves of an exploding bomb. Grace had become pregnant, but had lost the baby. A specialist came to our flat from the London Hospital to examine her and this was the only piece of news he could leave with us.

Only those who long to have children of their own, but cannot, will understand the pain we felt. We were totally in a daze. After the surgeon left, all we could do was to fall into each other's arms and weep, and the next few days were spent almost entirely trying to console one another.

The Bible records quite vividly the longing in people's hearts to have children. We have already looked at Abraham's cry to God for a child to be his heir, and there are many more examples. We see Rachel, desperate to bear Jacob's children, jealous of her sister who had already had four sons, crying out to her husband, "give me children or I'll die!" What pain, frustration and torment is discernible in that one phrase.

In the first chapter of the Book of Samuel the story of Hannah is recorded. She is one of two wives of a man called Elkanah. The other wife, Peninnah had children, but Hannah had none. Peninnah continually provoked Hannah, year after year, about her inability to bear children, until Hannah was reduced to tears and would not eat. This situation continued, and such was the torment she endured that we read these words in verses 10 to 11 of I Samuel. *"In bitterness of soul Hannah wept much and prayed to the Lord. And she made a vow, saying 'Oh Lord Almighty, if you will only look upon your servant's misery and remember me, and not forget your servant but give her a son, then I will give him to the Lord for all the days of his life'''*.

The Lord was gracious and answered Hannah's prayer. She gave birth to Samuel, who was given to Eli the priest to serve the Lord all his life. And there are many other examples of couples unable to have children; women who were, what the Bible rather painfully describes as barren.

There is little doubt that the great majority of married couples dream of having a family. The desperate measures many will go to is more than evident in our daily newspapers, when they discover that 'conventional' methods do not work. Fertility drugs, test-tube babies, and even surrogacy are just some of the avenues that they are prepared to go down in order to try and fulfil their longing for children of their own.

We knew the reason for the loss of the baby. Grace had a history of fybroids. While only two and a half years old she required an operation, and again at the age of twenty-four years. Now the problem had returned and the fybroids had killed the baby. Knowing the reason for the loss did not make it easier to accept.

Grace's parents were not Christians. Her father had been brought up a very religious man, but had never made a commitment to Christ. Because Grace was always ill as a baby, they were advised to move out of the City of London to a place where the air was cleaner. Consequently when she was two years old, they moved to Dagenham, Essex, the farthest out they could get at the time, because of her father's job.

By the time she was eleven years old, Grace had become a Christian through the witness of a schoolfriend, and was filled with the Holy Spirit at the age of thirteen years. Her mother objected to the 'religious mania' of her daughter, and only allowed her to attend church once a week. Because of the opposition at home to her new way of life, Grace could not read her Bible or pray unless she went out for a walk, usually around the local park.

The memory of one such walk came back to her in the midst of all the disappointment over the loss of the baby and the devastating news the specialist had brought. There was nothing different about the walk initially, but as she was taking her stroll around the park, God spoke to her quite clearly and told her she would marry an evangelist and would "live out of a suitcase". She knew then in her heart that God would one day use her in evangelism. At the same time, however, he seemed to ask her a question. "Are you prepared to give up everything for me?" Grace pondered for a moment. "Yes Lord, I will give up everything for you, but having a family. You wouldn't expect me to do that would you? After all, it is what you created us for isn't it?"

As the incident came flooding back into her mind, God spoke to her again. "Are you still willing to give up everything, even if you never have any children?"

Our disappointment turned to anger as we gave vent to our feelings. "What kind of God are you?," we cried. "We've given up everything for your sake and now you are asking this of us."

Our dream of having children and all the joy that entails lay shattered before us. In our hearts we were crying "why us?" We could not understand what purpose it would serve for us not to have children. Why did God seem to be asking this of us?

After pouring out all our anger, frustration and disappointment on the Lord, we came to a place of peace. We said yes to the Lord, but it cost a great deal, and we added this proviso. "If you are really asking this of us, we ask for your grace to accept it, but also for a spiritual family, sons and daughters in the Kingdom of God."

Some years later, in 1978, we knew for certain that any

hope at all that we had left of having children of our own was gone, when Grace was taken into hospital for a hysterectomy. Because she had already undergone so many operations already, her bowel collapsed and her condition became very serious indeed. The surgeon was not in the hospital at the time and was brought through London with a police escort to carryout the operation.

Grace was literally at death's door. At home folk were praying continually for her, while in the hospital two surgeons operated on her at the same time; one on the collapsed bowel and the other performing the hysterectomy. It was a miracle that she pulled through.

If nothing else, she has always been a fighter. She knew that after the operation it was up to each individual to make progress and so determined that she would be walking around the ward the day immediately after this major surgery. By 12 mid-day she had accomplished this and she was equally determined not to let what had happened demoralise her.

She began to go around the wards speaking to other patients and praying with them. The girl in the bed opposite her would boast about the fact that she had had two abortions, even though she was only seventeen years old, and her words were like a knife in Grace's heart. Grace admits that her first reaction to this girl was not entirely a Christian one. Then she realised that this young girl needed love and that she could not allow bitterness to take root in her own heart. She went across to her bed, and put her arms around her. Within a matter of seconds, the girl was weeping, what she had really wanted to do all the time. Her boasting was merely a cover for her true feelings. Even in the darkest moments such as these, God's light shone in and dispelled the clouds.

Our involvement with the young people at the Mission went a long way to answering our cry for spiritual sons and daughters. We had always enjoyed them, but after our moment of submission to the will of God, a break-through happened with regard to our relationship with them. We became like mum and dad to many of them, and they became a very important part of our lives. But this was not the total answer to our prayer.

The big turning point came for us when our good friends John and Chris Norton gave birth to a baby girl called Victoria. Once she was home from hospital, Chris involved us in almost every aspect of Victoria's life. We would often stay in their home overnight so we could enjoy being with her. In the mornings, Chris would feed her, then walk out of the room and leave us alone with her, to bathe her, cuddle, play with and generally enjoy her. When she was weaned, the first thing John and Chris did was to install a cot in our home, so that Victoria could stay overnight with us. They were excellent at drawing us into their family life, by simple acts such as allowing us to take Victoria to nursery school or go and buy things with her. Such unselfishness filled in huge gaps in our life.

The close involvement with Victoria was an immeasurable blessing, but we had to choose to touch areas where so many people without children get hurt. Just pushing someone else's child down the road in a pram could have been traumatic, but we learned to acknowledge our vulnerability, find God in our weakness and receive His blessing as a result.

Adapt or Adopt?

I called Sue, a young sixteen year old girl, into my vestry one day. In the meeting I had noticed that she looked very down in the mouth and wanted to find out if anything was wrong. She explained that her mother and step-father were emigrating to Australia and she did not wish to go with them. Even though she was not a Christian, Sue was fairly involved at the Mission. She was courting a young man

75

called Terry who she did not want to lose, and she had a job she did not wish to leave.

In one of those emotional moments that people experience, and they say things they later regret, I somehow communicated that if she ended up with nowhere to stay, Grace and I would be happy to have her live with us. Within a very short space of time, an angry mother was banging on our front door. "What do you think you are doing," she exploded as soon as I had let her into the house.

"What do you mean?", I asked, bewildered by this frontal attack.

"Sue has come home saying she doesn't have to go to Australia because Norman and Grace will look after her. What on earth gives you the right to interfere in our family life? I am trying to keep the family together and here you are doing exactly the opposite."

There was nothing left for me to do but eat humble pie and apologise.

At the same time as all of this was happening, my brother-in-law who worked for the Social Services, approached us about fostering a young girl. We were both reluctant. We had been through the process of trying to adopt a child, but because of our age difference, our poor income, and not owning our own home, we were turned down. We had often thought about fostering, but felt unable to cope with the emotional turmoil of caring for someone for a period of time, only to have to give them back. This was different, however. After my brother-in-law had explained that it was long term fostering, we agreed to go ahead.

The day before we were due to sign the fostering papers, Grace received a telephone call from a lady in our church. At the end of the conversation, the caller made a chance remark. "By the way, I hear you are going to have a young girl living with you."

"Oh, yes" said Grace, thinking about the girl we were about to foster.

"Susan's mum told me that you were having Susan to live with you."

Grace was totally amazed and could not believe what she had heard. It was my turn to move quickly and bang on Sue's mother's front door to ask what was going on.

"Oh yes" she replied to my questions, "we thought it was a good idea and decided to take you up on the offer."

We cancelled the fostering arrangements and within a short space of time, Sue moved in with us. The first year was hard going and a time of adapting for us all. We suddenly had a teenage girl thrust on us with all that means, and Sue had to get used to living with us and our hectic and very different lifestyle. One should never underestimate the difficulties involved for both parties in extended families.

Sue was not converted, but we put no pressure on her to become a Christian. We simply let her live, be a part of our life and observe. She was a bundle of problems. She had not had what she considered a good father and daughter relationship, found it difficult to relate to me, but desperately wanted to. We would sit talking for hours and eventually she came to trust me.

The year after she moved in, something remarkable happened in the Bible Class of about twenty to twenty-five young people. One Sunday I received a prophetic word from God for each member of the group. On the Monday evening Sue came home from work in a very quiet frame of mind. We recognised that God was speaking to her and said nothing. On Tuesday evening she came to us and said, "I've sorted it out. I want to become a Christian. Terry doesn't want to become a Christian, but I'm leaving him with that. I want to go on with God."

Within a day or two Terry contacted us and told us that he too wanted to become a Christian, and we had the joy of leading them both to the Lord. On the following Sunday they both gave their testimony at the meeting and over the next month twenty young people were saved, baptised in water and filled with the Holy Spirit.

Sue lived with us for three years, during which time she became as good as a daughter to us. We paid for her wedding and all the frills that accompany it and it was a joy to have Terry and Sue move into a house virtually opposite our own.

Before too long, Sue became pregnant. Another member of the Church asked her where Grace and I would fit into the picture when a child came along. "Of course," said Sue "they can choose what they want to be called, Nana or Grandma and Grandad." Now we are Grandma and Grandad to little Stephanie.

What's in a Name?

We had asked God for children and he had answered our prayer far in excess of what we could have expected. But something still niggled me. I could not shake it off, so after some deliberation I brought the matter before the Lord.

"Could I please have a son to carry on my name?" I asked. It was a seemingly ridiculous and impossible request, but by this time I felt so strongly about it, that I could do nothing else but pursue the thought with God.

In the twentieth century, and certainly in the western world, we have come to place very little value on names. In biblical times and still in certain cultures today, what a child is called is of considerable importance and either reflects something of its character, what its parents hope for it, or denotes its family, tribal or community ties. Even a desire for a son to be an heir and carry on the family name has lost some of its compulsion in the West. This may be due partly to the realisation that such an attitude has brought about feelings of inferiority in females and made women seem to be less important members of the community. Clearly in certain parts of the world, women are still regarded very much as second class citizens, due undoubtedly in no small measure to the fact that they do not carry on the family name once they are married.

I could not get away from the feeling, however, and ridiculous or not, I sought God for an answer.

In 1980 an Elder from the Church in Kwadaso called Daniel came to England and stayed for a month with Grace and myself. Mindful of all the generosity that I had experienced in Ghana, we gave of our best for him in terms of care and hospitality. While here, we went out and bought clothes for him and helped him to buy clothes for his wife Mary.

In 1981 we visited Ghana again. As usual, we were treated with great kindness and received with warmth and love. At one point during our stay we were approached by David Mills, who said, "Norman, you've got a problem."

"Oh, what's that," I replied.

"Daniel and Mary have been talking together. They were so blessed by the way you looked after Daniel when he was in England, and your love and care for them, they want to give you a gift."

I cannot do justice in words to the feelings that I experienced at that moment. Again and again we were moved by the generosity of a people who have so little, yet are willing to sacrifice everything to bless others. Nothing, however, had prepared me for David's next words.

"Yes. They feel that as you have no children of your own, they would like to give you their youngest son."

I could hardly take in what I had heard. The import of what David was saying took my breath away. I knew that this was not just a gesture, but a serious offer from a couple who had obviously grown to appreciate Grace and myself and wanted to show their thanks in a way that they thought would bless us most. This too from Ghanaians who hold their children very dear. The whole thing was too much for me and, not for the first time in my travels to Ghana, I was reduced to tears.

Ghanaian law would not have allowed me to bring the child out of the country. Whether I would have actually done so if it had been permissible is doubtful. Although I was thrilled and overwhelmed by the immensity of the gift, I would not have wanted to tear the child totally out of his culture and all that was familiar to him. I left him in Ghana, but Grace and I could echo the words of Isaiah in more ways than one, "to us a son is given."

After our return to England, I received a letter from Daniel in which was the following news:

"Your son is doing well. His name was Ebenezer, but now he is old enough to talk and understand what we have told him about you, he refuses to answer to that name. He wishes only to be called Norman Barnes and that is now his adopted name."

Later I also heard from Nicholas Andoh, my first contact in Ghana. His wife had also given birth to a son who they had decided to call Norman Barnes.

Grace was not to be left out. Another of the Elders in Kwadaso had increased the size of his family by one in the form of another little girl. Because the tradition in Ghana is to name children after people you appreciate, Johnny and his wife already had a small David and Margaret Mills running around the house. All the pressure was on the couple, however, to call this little girl by the grandmother's name. Johnny turned the suggestion down and flatly refused to even entertain the idea. The grandmother was dead, and he did not want his daughter named after a dead person, but after somebody who he appreciated and who was alive.

Over a period of time he had come to a deep appreciation for "Mammy Barnes" because Grace, a white woman, had gone out to Ghana and had showed them all love, care and concern. "I want to call my little daughter after Mammy Barnes."

It was a moving and thrilling time for Grace, at the dedication of the baby in the church, as she heard the name Grace Barnes officially given to the little girl.

God had heard our cry and given us nephews and nieces, children and grandchildren, and three little Africans named after us.

When we first heard that we were not going to be able to have children, we were devastated. This was not helped by a remark from a thoughtless individual who informed us it was God's judgement on us for leaving a certain church. Since that time we have come across many couples who have struggled with the stresses, frustration and heartache that childlessness brings. Because of all our experiences we have been able to sympathise and relate to them much more easily, offering counsel and advice based on our own walk through the valley of despair. More than this, the measure of how much God has filled in the emptiness in our lives and answered our prayers much more than we could ever have dreamed of, is evidenced many times in our ministry to such couples. We are sometimes given prophetic words by the Holy Spirit for these people, telling them that they will have children and that they are to trust the word of the Lord for them. The remarkable thing about this is, that such is the work that God has done in our lives, that we are able to give this information and rejoice with the couple concerned, without feeling resentment or jealousy. This is not to say that at times we still do not feel the hurt of not having our very own children. There are moments when we get caught out, for example because a conversation is predominantly about children, and such moments affect us emotionally. But there is a difference between hurting and weeping, which I feel is legitimate and necessary, and getting bitter and hardened about the matter.

At the same time as I received a letter from Daniel telling me of my son, John and Chris Norton were also expecting another child. When Chris went into hospital, Grace and I moved into their home to help take care of the household and look after the family. One evening, after the little boy was born, as we all sat around the tea-table, John spoke.

"We have decided on a name for the baby. we are going to call him Simon."

"That's nice" I said.

"But we want to give him another name - Barnes. We would like to call him Simon Barnes Norton. We want him to have your name because of our relationship and close friendship, and when he grows up, I'll explain to him why he has your name. I want my son to have your name."

As we sat there, thrilled by this gesture from our two close friends, I was aware that the Lord was speaking to me.

"Son, I have more than one way of answering prayer."

Chapter 5
Land of Dreams

It took the early Church a while to adjust. The man who had been leading a fierce persecution against them, dragging them off to prison, was suddenly standing up in public places proclaiming that Jesus was indeed the Christ, the Lord. Saul, who changed his name to Paul, had clearly undergone such a dramatic conversion that he found no real problem in announcing the good news that had brought such a turn-about in his life.

The man was fired up. He had met with the risen Christ, had received a commission and was determined to waste no time. This sudden change not only caught the first Christians by surprise; Paul's erstwhile companions and fellow persecutors were undoubtedly not a little taken aback. It was not too long before both groups realised that his conversion was real and the former accepted him, albeit with a little caution, into their midst, while the latter sought to find him and take his life.

I am sure that Paul was ready to take on the world. His whole view of life changed and nothing could have seemed so important to him as to begin spreading the good news of new life in Christ. He had been commissioned as the Apostle to the Gentiles, and the dream was born in his heart of reaching the known world with the gospel. God, however, was not in so much of a hurry as his latest follower.

We read in Galatians chapter two how Paul disappeared from public view for a while and spent a number of years in the deserts of Arabia. It is almost certain those years were times of learning, receiving instruction and some of the tremendous revelation that was later to become part of Paul's teaching ministry and would eventually form a large part of our New Testament.

Those desert years were important. They were a vital part of the shaping of Paul, and only when they were over could he begin to see his dream fulfilled. The stories of Paul's travels are well documented and for a man who did not have the benefit of air travel and fast cars, he certainly affected significant areas of the world for the Kingdom of God. You can almost feel the burning desire in the man's heart in the account in the Book of Acts; sense the urging in his heart to press ever further into other lands and situations with the liberating Gospel of Jesus Christ. A man with a dream in his heart, a commission to fulfil, and a goal to achieve. The words that seem to have been branded in his heart were ''I press on ... I press on.''

By the end of 1985, I felt that God was beginning to open up the way for me to see my dream of reaching the world fulfilled. Looking back over the previous ten years, I could see that in some respects there had been an 'Arabian' experience for me. We had received many blessings, but had also learnt a lot, had our lives and characters shaped, and above all discovered the meaning of serving one another, caring, committed relationships, true friendship and what it means to be part of the family of God.

I could look back on the last two years and remember trips to Ghana, India and America that significantly affected my life, but also opened up further doors of opportunity to serve and help care for people. I was excited about the possibilities that seemed to be coming our way and none more so than in February 1986.

We were in a plane high above the Atlantic, flying towards the continent of America. There would still be many hours before we would reach our destination. We had eaten a good meal and were settling down for the rest of the flight, excited about the prospect of our first visit to Texas.

It was my third and Grace's second visit to the States. The first for me had been a fairly low-key affair. I had travelled with another member of the ministry team to which I belonged, called Team Spirit, headed up by John Noble, to a group of churches that had been given the nick-name "The Move". A large number of the people involved with The Move were based on farms spread around America, indeed in a number of countries around the world, and the trip was, therefore, a series of visits to different farming communities.

As I sat on the plane, quietly gazing out of the window, I began to think about America, the circumstances of my second trip, when Grace had accompanied me, and the subsequent events that had led to the decision to go for a third time.

I will always be grateful to the Lord that he took me to Ghana before America. There is something about the States that appeals to me immensely. The lifestyle and much of what I had experienced seemed to fit in so well with my out-going personality and love of action. Ghana brought me down to earth and made me realise that two-thirds of the world lived like the Ghanaians, not like the Americans, and in all my enjoyment of the resources, facilities and abundance of America, Ghana served to continually remind me of the need of the majority of people on earth. This did not stop me enjoying myself whilst in America, however, and certainly did not seem to hinder the Holy Spirit doing his work.

For many, America is the land of dreams. The Statue of Liberty is a great symbol of the freedom millions have come to enjoy, along with the prosperity of a thriving nation. This abundance has of course brought its problems as well as blessings, and like everywhere else, prosperity is not for everyone.

My dream for America was along different lines. I was keen to find out what God was doing and meet people who were enjoying some of the new things that were taking place with the move of the Holy Spirit world-wide.

Our second trip in 1985 had involved a visit to California

to meet a girl called Robin Williams. On our way back we had arranged to call in at a place called Russellville, Arkansas. We had a fairly long-standing relationship with some of the people in the fellowship in Russellville and it was great to be able to spend a short time with them. We were asked to speak at one of their meetings. At that particular period, the leadership felt that they wanted to keep the meetings reasonably short, but as our time together began, I became convinced that God wanted us to do something different. I turned to the man in charge of the meeting and said, "please give me time. I know God wants to move among us in a special way."

I had already decided that I would share on the subject of "Dreams and Visions", and as I began to speak people started to weep openly. I felt compelled to go out towards certain couples in the meeting and speak what God had given to me for them. It was a real step of faith. Some of the things I had to say were very precise, but by people's reactions, I knew that I must have heard God correctly.

One couple was extremely fearful about their baby. They felt the Lord was going to test their faith by taking the baby away from them. I stood with them against this lie. We were also able to prophesy over six ladies who were widows about their future ministry and the people God had given them to serve.

One woman that I spoke to I saw clearly in my mind sitting in her kitchen. I had no idea why, but I knew that she felt that what she was doing was insignificant. It turned out that she was someone who had 'open house', her back door was always open, and the kitchen was the place where she did all her counselling. As I shared God's appreciation of what she was doing, she seemed to be amazed that God knew so much about her.

We closed the meeting officially but carried on ministering to people, bringing them words of prophecy and encouragement. The idea of a short meeting was soon forgotten by the leaders as people queued up to be prayed for. It was our first real experience of such an overwhelming response and we were amazed as we laid hands on people and found the Holy Spirit giving us words of knowledge for everyone for whom we prayed.

It was gratifying once we were back in England to receive a letter from one of those we prayed for which said, among other things, "you will never know what a comfort your ministry was to me. If it were not for your word to me, I would have gone insane, due to the difficulties I was facing at the time."

From Russellville we travelled to Little Rock, another town in Arkansas, to spend some time with an old friend by the name of Peter Parris. Peter was heading up a growing work in the area and had become something of a "first amongst equals" for a number of leaders. He had arranged a Retreat for a few of those leaders and myself whilst we were in the area, to be held on a farm a short car ride from his home.

There were five of us on the Retreat. Peter and I had a room of our own for the night, while the other three slept in the lounge together. In the middle of the night, about 2.00 a.m., I woke up and sensed that God wanted to speak to me. As I lay waiting on the Lord, I felt the Holy Spirit impress on me that I needed to serve the others on the Retreat, by washing their feet. "But Lord," I protested, "that is ridiculous. It has absolutely no cultural relevance. What is this all about?"

In spite of my protestations, the feeling would not leave me that this is what I had to do. "Well, all I can say is" I continued, "I am not going around looking for a bucket and that is final. There is no bowl in the sink because they use dishwashers."

Hardly had the words escaped from my mouth when my eyes went to the corner of the room. There in all its glory was a wash stand with an old-fashioned pitcher and basin.

My heart sank, but so did my will. I understood then why I had been given this particular room and reluctantly I gave in to the Lord. I felt that God also gave me some prophetic words to speak to the others and finally, with all these things established in my heart, I went back to sleep.

The next morning, as I entered the kitchen, Peter Parris was cooking breakfast for us all.

"What are we going to do today Norman?" he asked.

"Peter, I've got one or two things I would like to do. The Lord woke me up in the night and spoke to me, and if you are happy, I would like to share those things. Oh, and there is one particular thing I need to do."

Peter happily agreed. After we had eaten breakfast together he asked, "well, Norman, what do you feel?"

I recounted the events of the previous night, still feeling slightly embarrassed about what I was proposing to do. "All I can say to you is, I have got to use the pitcher and washbasin to wash your feet. I don't understand what it means. It seems to have no relevance at all to me, although I have heard of Christians doing it in other countries, but I feel so strongly that this is what God has said I must do. So if you are willing, I would like to do that."

None of the men present objected and so I went to Peter Parris with the washbasin and a towel in my hands. After kneeling in front of him, I removed his shoes and socks. "I feel such a fool" was all I could say. I rinsed his feet and dried them, praying and speaking in tongues as I did so. I reminded myself of the fact that the Lord had done the same for his disciples, and although I did not understand why he had asked me to do this, I would gladly obey him.

As I got to the second man and began to do the same, the reality of what I was doing hit me. The picture of Jesus washing feet came into sharp focus and reduced me to weeping. By the time I reached the third man, I could have washed his feet with my tears, my eyes were like fountains. I broke out into uncontrollable sobs, hardly able to see because my eyes were now considerably swollen. I washed his feet, and staggered to the last man, but found I could not kneel or stand, I was just an emotional heap on the floor. Somehow I managed to wash his feet and then tried to move towards my chair. I could not get up to sit in it, and so I knelt beside it and sobbed the deepest sobs I have ever done in my life.

I felt God had revealed in a fresh way the truth of laying down our lives for the brethren. I did not feel humiliated at what had taken place, but deeply humbled. Even though what I had done was menial and totally foreign to me, I did not feel a fool any more for having done it. I was overwhelmed by what God had done for me and what he had enabled and privileged me to do for others. In those brief moments I saw Jesus, the son of God as the son of man, who had emptied himself of all his glory to become a human being and I felt totally unworthy. To say that my emotions and feelings were all mixed up would be an understatement!

The next thing I became aware of was that the other men in the room were gathering around me. ''Not just because you've done it to us'' one said, ''but because we feel you are worthy of it, we would like to wash your feet.''

They proceeded to do this, but it was not too long before they were reduced to the same emotional state as I was in. As we were gathered in this way I began to pray and prophecy over them and found God gave me a word that was very relevant for each one. The Lord had certainly broken in on the Retreat and done all the planning.

As we prayed for each other, one of the men said, ''Norman, I know you have a burden for the world. I have the strongest feeling that God will take you to mainland China.'' Everyone else seemed to agree totally with this. In the natural it was not possible, for I had no contacts either in China or in Britain that I knew of, but I responded positively to this word. ''I receive that from the Lord,'' I said, ''God has done so many other things for me, I believe he will get me to mainland China.''

The trip had been an eventful one, both in terms of seeing people blessed and challenged by the prophetic word of God, but also in my encounter with Jesus, the Son of Man, through the simple act of washing those men's feet. I was not going to forget too quickly, either, the word concerning China.

Not long after I returned to England I received a letter from an old friend, a pastor of an Elim church called Brian Richardson. He told me about a couple called Charles and Paula Slagle that he had invited over to England, because he felt we needed their ministry. That immediately put me on my guard.

Brian had sent all the literature that this couple had given him about their ministry and I have to say that I was not in the least bit impressed by it. They did not seem to be anything special to me and I was wary about claims of ''unique'' ministry at the best of times. But somehow I could not lose the feeling that we should have them. In the end I decided we would risk it and have them at the Mission for the Saturday night and Sunday meetings. At the worst it would be a weekend to quickly forget!

The Saturday evening came and our folk dutifully arrived at the hall for the meeting. As I walked in I saw all the P.A. equipment being set up and my heart sank a little bit further. I asked Charles and Paula to come into the vestry so that we could pray together. After everyone had introduced themselves, we prayed and as they opened up their hearts to God, I felt a warmth towards them.

We had decided that our people would lead the worship for a while and then hand over to Charles and Paula to do whatever they wanted to do. Before we had hardly started to praise God, I looked across to see the Slagles both crying. They were obviously moved and once again I felt a warmth towards them. Very shortly after that the Lord gave me a prophecy for them, so I stopped the meeting and gave the word to them. It turned out to be a fairly accurate appraisal of what they had been experiencing, but also contained promises that God was about to confirm the word he had given to them (whatever that was!).

After this we gave the meeting over to them and settled down to listen. The first half of their ministry was much as we had expected. They sang well together, using backing tracks to enhance the quality of their songs, but their style of music was not exactly what we were used to and I was not particularly impressed. I consoled myself with the thought that at the very least we would have had a bit of Saturday night entertainment.

Then Charles sat down at his synthesiser and asked one of the young men in the congregation to stand up. Trevor was one of our leaders, and one of the most sensitive at that. Charles began to sing out a prophecy to him and as he did so, the atmosphere became electric. He opened up Trevor's life story like a book. It was the most incredible word of knowledge I had ever heard. As I looked around, everyone was moved to tears.

Charles moved on to other people and it soon became obvious that here was a man who was really in tune with the Holy Spirit, for the details he was revealing about different members of the congregation were so accurate and so encouraging they left us all astounded. As he spoke into lives, he gave faith, hope and in some cases, tremendous promises.

On Sunday morning we cancelled all our home groups and told everyone to meet at the Mission to hear the Slagles. It was a different story to Saturday night. Whereas no-one wanted to be picked the night before, now everyone leaned forward in their seats trying to catch Charles' eye, desperate to hear from God themselves. It was quite amusing to see people trying to catch his attention without looking too obvious.

We needed no more convincing about the authenticity of Brian Richardson's claims and the uniqueness of this ministry we had experienced. Over a period of time, during which we loved and cared for the Slagles, we became firm friends with them. We invited them back to England on a number of occasions, when their ministry gained wider recognition and their humour and friendliness, as well as their ability to bring the word of the Lord to people, placed them in popular demand. So close did we become that eventually the Mission office became the agency for handling their ministry in the U.K.

Charles also had a number of things to say to Grace and myself which he felt were from God. One of them was that we would stand before kings and high authorities and be able to share the word of God. To some extent this has already been fulfilled. Another very significant word was that we were to move in words of knowledge in a similar way to Charles and Paula and that our ministry would be a ministry of tears.

Before you can have a ministry of tears, you have to know what it is to weep yourself. I am reminded of how concerned John Wesley became, because he had not wept for a certain number of days. Certainly God has taken Grace and me through the valley of tears on more than one occasion in our own experience, and it has been our joy and privilege to see Charles' word to us fulfilled. In the last three years, in every meeting we have ministered in, someone has been moved to tears by the touch of God on their lives.

Land of Tears

I received an invitation from Charles to visit Texas where he and Paula live and share in some of the churches with whom he had a relationship. Apparently he had written to all the leaders explaining how we had become friends and asking them to allow us to minister some of the things that God had placed in our hearts over the years.

Such an invitation was not to be ignored. Grace and I made plans to travel. Then disaster struck. I had been having problems for some time with my voice when speaking. I was constantly having to stop and take drinks to soothe my throat. After an examination by the doctor, I was told that I required an operation if I wanted to continue being a preacher, and soon! I explained about my forthcoming visit to Texas, to which the doctor replied that the only way to fulfil that commitment would be to have the operation immediately, and then not speak one word for a whole week in order to allow the throat to recover quickly and properly.

As much as the thought of a week's total silence seemed somewhat daunting, I agreed. The operation was carried out, and for a whole week I communicated by pad and pen, sign language and facial expression. Anyone who knows me will understand what a trial that was.

Several people were concerned that I should be going to Texas to carry out a heavy preaching tour so soon after the operation. I was prepared to cancel the trip, but as I prayed about it, felt we should go on as planned.

My musing and thoughts on the plane had brought us much closer to our destination. As I came back to the present, the plane was preparing to descend, and we fastened our seat belts, ready to land. Our third visit was about to begin. We had little idea of what awaited us. The people we would meet were from a totally different background to what we had been used to for the past nine or ten years. We were excited, however, about the whole trip and looked forward to being able to share on some of the subjects that Charles had requested us to minister on, such as community, covenant relationships and commitment.

Our first stop was in the town of Azle, near Forth Worth. This was the sort of place that rarely asked other people to come and speak: they were quite satisfied with the ministry that they received regularly and faithfully from their own pastor. On the recommendation of Charles Slagle, however,

Grace and I were given an invitation.

Prayer breakfasts and breakfast meetings are very popular in the States, something that has never really caught on in England to the same extent. It was to such a meeting that I was first asked to speak. It was a jovial time, with plenty of good humour and laughter and after a substantial breakfast I was introduced and asked to speak to the men present. I spoke about the qualities of leadership, and as I continued I was aware of a sort of hush descending on the gathering. It was clear that the Holy Spirit was stirring these men and causing them to think about what was being said and it was a good start to the trip.

On the Sunday I shared about relationships and used examples such and Ruth and Naomi and David and Jonathan to show that the covenant type relationship always produces Christ. After this we started to move out to people, praying for them and prophesying into their lives. We began to see very clearly the fulfilment of Charles Slagle's prophetic word to us concerning a ministry of tears.

We spoke to one family that apparently was back-slidden. Through the word of knowledge we were able to describe how God saw the man's relationship to his wife and children. Before we had gone too far the man just seemed to break like a bursting dam and as a result a healing process was begun.

We then prayed for a young couple whom we sensed were going through a tough time. They too began to cry. I felt I should prophesy to a certain man in the congregation, and so told him that God was going to exalt him even though he had been through a very low time. Little did I know at the time that the man had been a millionaire, but his business had gone bust. As I stood with him, I suddenly became aware that the husband of the young couple I had spoken to before was this man's son.

"God wants you two to be reconciled," I said, "There needs to be a renewing of your relationship." I brought father and son together and it did not take too long before they were openly weeping on each other's shoulder. This affected everyone present and looking around, there was hardly a dry eye in the place.

I realised that there was also something not quite right between daughter and mother-in-law, and so brought the two of them together. It was a very moving moment to see all four people sobbing in the aisle together.

We prophesied over so many, both young and old, and again and again the result was the same; people breaking down and weeping, being reconciled to one another and God. Every night of the four nights we spent in Azle, the scene was the same. Sometimes the hush of the Holy Spirit would come upon the meeting like a gentle breeze and no one dared to move. It was quite remarkable how God blessed His people.

On the last day Kerry Wood, the pastor, asked me to speak to all the leaders. We met at 6.00 a.m. for another breakfast session. ''Norman'' Kerry asked ''please share with us the cost of all you have been talking about.''

I spoke about the hurts that are inevitable in any serious relationship. There would always be misunderstandings, mistakes and miscommunication that will cause problems. I found myself moved as I looked out on this group of men with a genuine hunger for the things of God and a real desire to learn. ''Once you have seen the blessing that committed relationships bring,'' I said ''nothing less will satisfy. You will not be able to go back and accept a more superficial involvement with people.'' So many pastors, I felt, did not know what it meant to have deep, lasting friendships. They were placed on a pedestal by the congregation, given a title of pastor, and as leaders were expected to live an almost perfect life. There was no place for them to share their weaknesses or vulnerability; no one, apart from their marriage partner, to unburden their problems and needs on. If they had any special friends, it could so easily be regarded as favouritism. The result was that there were a large number of them trying to bear the burden of this status that had been thrust upon them, which God never intended them to carry.

Before I had finished, all of us, without exception, were weeping. As we glimpsed the possibilities and joys, as well as the hurts, that true friendship and a committed relationship brings, we were filled with hope and thankfulness to God that we were part of the same family and would, in pursuing this vision, see Christ revealed in His Body, the Church, on the earth.

Confident that our visit to Azle would not be our last, we moved on to Granbury, a town just outside Dallas. The pastor there was Dave Leatherwood, a man who was working hard to build the church and bring about a good core of leadership.

The time spent in this church was as remarkable as the previous four days in Azle. Once again, as we moved out to pray for people, God gave us specific words that went straight to the heart of their situation and circumstances at the time.

I noticed one man sitting at the back of the church. "You need to get out of the back row and sit at the front," I said to him, to which the whole church responded. I subsequently found out that he had been asked to be involved in leadership but had responded by saying, "no, I'm not worthy."

Without knowing anything about their circumstances, we were led to speak to two other men about the fact that God wanted them in positions of responsibility, and it turned out that they too had been asked to join the leadership team but had refused on the same grounds as the first man we had spoken to.

The meeting continued in this vein, with words of knowledge being given for a good number of people. I felt I had finished and began walking down the aisle to the front of the church. Out of the corner of my eye I saw a man on the end of one of the rows, spun round and said to him some very simple words. "The Lord says to you, well done, good and faithful servant." As I finished the sentence, it was as if someone had hit him with a sledge hammer. He fell foward onto me and sobbed his heart out. He felt he had not been recognised for all the time and effort he had given to the church, but was in fact probably the most faithful servant in the whole fellowship.

What a thrill it is to obey the leading of the Lord and be faithful to those things he tells you to do. So often we look for powerful words to speak to people, when often the very simple things are what they need. On numerous occasions we were surprised by the effect our words had. Often they seemed so ordinary to us, yet they were absolutely 'right on the button' for the people concerned and brought joy, release, repentance and healing.

From Granbury we moved onto Houston where we experienced much the same as in the previous two churches and finally our tour ended up in Laredo, a city right on the border of Mexico. In fact, 95% of the population is Mexican.

The vitality, enthusiasm and the culture of the Mexican people appealed to me immensely and so I was a little confused by the apparent inability to respond to the worship music that seemed lively and 'Mexican' enough. As soon as the calypso rhythm started up, I found it quite easy to respond in dance accordingly. Everyone around me, however, seemed to be jumping up and down on one foot.

"I do not understand this," I told them. "This cannot be right. There is so little real expression of who you are. Surely there must be a place for your style of dance in your worship."

It was explained to me that many of the people were a little nervous of being true to their culture because they were not really sure how to direct that style of dancing to the Lord.

But I encouraged them to be themselves and just remain sensitive to the Holy Spirit.

Unbeknown to me, they planned a particular song for the meeting on the next evening. As soon as I walked into the building they played it and immediately I started to dance. Before I knew what was happening, people were out dancing in true Mexican style, worshipping God in a way that was appropriate to them, and not an effort to conform to another culture. It was a great thrill to see so many people released into praising God in this way.

Once again, in all the meetings in Laredo, the Lord moved among us in a sovereign way, giving words of knowledge for many people. So profuse were the words in fact, that by the end of the meetings, people were clapping and cheering.

Very quickly we formed a good relationship with the pastors of the church, Norman and Sandra Howell. We had certain things in common which may well have drawn us close to each other, such as the fact that they were unable to have children of their own. But whatever the reasons, we clicked as couples easily and naturally. So good was our relationship, in fact, that Grace invited Sandra to England to speak at a womens retreat that she was planning.

At one point during one of the meetings I felt I should get Norman and Sandra, who were seated in the congregation, and bring them to the front. There were about 300 people present. I stood the pair of them in front of their own congregation and said, "this couple needs to know that you love them."

For a few moments there was complete silence and then one man stood up and clapped. Others followed suit, until the whole thing began to snowball. In the end, everyone was standing and clapping wildly and went on and on for between ten and fifteen minutes.

Suddenly, like a breath of wind had blown across the congregation, the applause stopped. There was absolute silence again. A man came out from the congregation, stood before Norman and Sandra, then broke down and cried. Everyone in the congregation started to weep. At this point Grace and I went to a corner of the platform to sit down and watch. One by one people came out and put their arms around the couple and through great sobs, told them that they loved them. It took three-quarters of an hour to go through this, but it was not a moment too long. It was a privilege to experience such a scene and I have no doubt in my mind that many a leader would like to be on the receiving end of such an expression of love and care, even if it were a little embarrassing.

So ended our third trip to America. It was probably the most fulfilling ministry we had experienced up to that time. We were thrilled by the response and the way God met people through words of knowledge and prophecy. As my dream of reaching the world had unfolded just that little bit more, so I realised that the way we could serve in each country would probably be different. In Ghana we had been able to help very much in the material realm, providing some of the basic necessities of life as well as a few luxuries. In America we had shared some of the principles the Lord had built into our lives over the years such as commitment, friendship and covenant relationship. I became excited again about all that God had spoken to me about concerning the world; the words I had received from various people about going to different countries, and all the possibilities this would open up in terms of being able to serve the Body of Christ in a variety of ways.

Fruit that will Last

Seeing dreams fulfilled brings responsibility and accountability. I have always admired the Apostle Paul for his tireless devotion to the churches he had helped to establish, a number of whom I might have been tempted to give up on. Throughout the pages of much of the New

Testament, we cannot fail to sense the burning desire in the man's heart to reach the world for Christ. He made use of every opportunity to present the Gospel and stayed for long periods in different cities and regions to try and establish a thriving church, even though he often experienced considerable opposition and persecution.

He did not, however, move onto another part of the world and just forget the church or churches he had been involved with. Many times we read that he revisited them in order to encourage, teach, correct, strengthen and establish good leadership. He was keen to see that everything was proceeding in the right way, that correct building was taking place on the foundations he had laid. Often his return visits would be as lengthy or longer than his first, and during these times he worked hard and gave himself sacrificially to the particular church. To the church in Corinth he wrote, *"now I am ready to visit you for the third time, and I will not be a burden to you ... I will very gladly spend for you everything I have and expend myself as well."*

Paul did not just set the ball rolling in a particular place and then leave town once the successful evangelistic thrust had been completed. He felt responsible and acted responsibly towards those he had helped into the Kingdom of God. He knew his dream meant accountability to God for what happened in the infant churches and he did his level best to ensure that he fulfilled his commission completely.

On our return from the States we received encouraging news. One pastor wrote to us saying "in your four days with us, we feel as though we have moved forward two years." Such comments certainly gave us confidence in the ministry God had placed in our hands and faith and a sense of anticipation for what the future held. We were concerned, however, that we were responsible about what we had ministered. In the state that is traditionally known as the land of the cowboys, we did not want to become ministry cowboys who rode in, shot up the town and left the pastor to clean up afterwards. We wanted to be held accountable for the things we had said to so many people.

Early in 1987 we returned to Texas to check out if our words had actually borne any fruit. If the words had been of God, we had no need to fear.

We flew into Houston to spend five days with the Church of Living Water, with a congregation of between 150 to 200 people, pastored by Bryan Morrison. They had experienced a difficult time, as had all of Texas, because of the slump in the economy and several members had been forced to move away to find work, while others were working on minimum time.

In many ways we felt that on our previous visit, our time in Houston had seen the least happen, yet it was obvious on our return that much more had taken place than we had realised. We were greeted warmly and immediately reminded of everything we had shared with them. It was tremendous to see families still rejoicing in the word given to them the previous year, having experienced a new beginning in different areas of their lives. What a joy to see so much ongoing fruit.

Whilst there Grace had an opportunity to preach in a main meeting, which was enthusiastically received and I spoke one evening on world mission, using the now rather unimaginative title of 'The world, our parish'. Once again we experienced the Holy Spirit breaking in on the situation, and as the challenge went out to consider the opportunities to serve God that existed in so many parts of the world, so people were visibly moved.

As we came to the end of the meeting, Bryan Morrison, through great sobs said, "I love all of you, but the time is coming when I will leave and not come back. God has put the world in my heart and I must go." So affected was he by what God had spoken to him that he could not close the meeting. He simply stood there crying, repeating those words.

We were to experience this scene over and over again in almost every church we visited and I believe it was but a reflection of the desire of many leaders who want, and need, to be released from their local setting to wider situations, preferably overseas, if only for short periods.

From Houston we moved on to Granbury, near Dallas. It was good to see how God had begun to really bless the work of David and Beverley Leatherwood after four years faithful service. The church commenced a week of prayer at the beginning of January and such was the presence of the Lord that it had continued every night right through into March when we arrived. Coming into such an atmosphere was a bit special.

Strangely, in spite of this obvious blessing, the church was at a crossroads financially. They had $19 in the bank and bills of $1400 that had to be paid by the following Monday. There was no money for bills and certainly none for us! Fortunately, we were not too thrown by this state of affairs, even though we were sailing close to the wind financially ourselves on the trip. God had been speaking to me before our arrival in Dallas, reminding me that he was the source of our financial wellbeing, not America.

On the Sunday morning, one day before the bills were due to be paid, they took up an offering totalling $3000, which covered all the immediate problems more than adequately. I ministered again on world mission and the response was almost exactly the same as it had been at Houston. David just stood in front of the congregation and wept continuously, unable to speak. He could not close the meeting and did not seem to know what to do. Nobody moved, even though the meeting was almost at an end. No-one seemed to want to go. Finally, he pulled himself together to be able to speak.

"In Norman's ministry we have heard about the incredible generosity of the Ghanaians in spite of their abject poverty. I feel the least we can do as a relatively prosperous people, is to take up another offering for Norman and Grace.''

As a result we received $650 and with grateful hearts, were able to reaffirm that God is indeed our source and the one who meets our needs.

Whilst in Dallas we stayed on a small hundred acre ranch where another of my dreams was fulfilled. I am so glad that God is not just concerned with fulfilling the large dreams we hold in our hearts, or those that are directly concerned, as we would see it, with the work of His Kingdom. I was taught to ride a real quarter-horse. This is nothing like English riding and the riding position is something else. The horse is highly trained and very sensitive and the saddle is much deeper. No bobbing up and down on those horses!

Next we travelled to Azle and our dear friends Kerry and Faith Wood. We arrived right in the middle of a big dispute. Several changes were taking place in the life of the church, especially with regard to church government, worship and finance. Unfortunately all this caused a split with the resultant tears and heartaches. Kerry was having to leave with two-thirds of the congregation wishing to go with him.

We arrived in the last week of their time in the church building and were asked to approach the congregation on the basis of ''this is the new church, put foundations into us for the future.'' As a result we felt very strongly to encourage them to be flexible, to look at everything they did and ask God how he felt about it all.

Again I shared about world mission and Kerry experienced the same as the other leaders. God is so clearly preparing his people to reach out and touch the world in an unprecedented fashion.

During our stay in Azle, yet another of my smaller dreams was fulfilled, although for a boy from Dagenham it still seemed pretty unlikely. I was taken to a rodeo, and it was better than I ever expected. Of one thing I am sure, however, I would not ride a bucking horse or bull for a pension!

We spent a few days at the home of Charles and Paula Slagle to rest and enjoy one another's company. While there we had the opportunity to fly to Los Angeles for twenty-four hours with the Slagles, who were appearing on a T.V. show. Yet another of my dreams was fulfilled. As we walked out of the airport, transport was waiting to whisk us away to the T.V. studios. I had a ride in one of those long limousines and felt just like a character from T.V. myself.

We visited two churches we had not been to on our first trip. In Austin we were received extremely warmly and asked if we could return again at some time. The other new contact was a church called Eagle's Nest in Charles and Paula's home town of San Antonio.

Eagle's Nest has grown from nothing to a membership of 2000 in four years. Rick Godwin was the pastor of a very large, successful church, but felt he should start Eagle's Nest. Now they have bought a large area in a shopping precinct, which would normally be used for a supermarket, and turned it into a church building.

Before we ministered, we were called out by the leaders who wanted to pray for us. The day prior to this meeting, Grace had suffered with incredible pain in her back. I had prayed for her and the pain had eased a little, but she was still in considerable discomfort. Nobody at Eagle's Nest knew about it. As the leaders gathered around us to pray, one of them said to Grace, "I would like to pray for your back," and as a result of that prayer the pain disappeared completely.

They prophesied into our lives about our marriage with such encouraging words, and naturally Grace and I were reduced to tears. Then I was told by one man I would be going to Russia, which was the fourth time I had been given that word. To Grace they prophesied she would be a teacher among women with a ministry to thousands, and then came a word that set my heart soaring. "The Lord knows your burden about healing and seeing people come out of wheelchairs. The day when you will see this is closer than you could imagine." How I thank God that my dream of many years was still very much in his heart too and that before too long I would begin to see it fulfilled.

Once again, as we ministered, people were moved by the Spirit of God. Words of knowledge brought tears, release and healing. As we prophesied over people, so the rest of the congregation were clapping, cheering and stomping. They were not content with quiet 'amens' and polite murmurs of approval, and some of their enthusiasm and responsiveness would not go amiss in some of our congregations in England.

Our last port of call was Laredo and the church led by Norman and Sandra Howell. Many have moved into new areas of covenant life, exploring what it means to be a community of believers in the truest sense, and for some this has been at great cost. But what a delight it was to see such solid fruit remaining from our previous ministry.

Looking back over our two trips to Texas, it appears to be a never ending round of tears and weeping. This is, of course, a slight exaggeration, for there were many times of hilarity, rejoicing and laughter. I believe, however, that all the tears we saw and experienced ourselves were the fulfilment of God's word to us through Charles and Paula Slagle concerning a ministry of tears.

As much as many people in England might feel uncomfortable with such obvious displays of emotion, I believe that they are very important. With the tears comes release and thereafter can follow healing. How sad it would be if we in England let our so called stiff upper lip prevent us from entering into the blessing that God has for us.

I am so glad that the characters in the Bible were not English. The men felt no shame to cry. King David wrote *"all night long I flood my bed with weeping and drench my couch with tears"* (Psalm 6 v 6).

He was also convinced God took account of our tears for in Psalm 56 v 8 we read *"record my lament, list my tears in your scroll, are they not in your record?"*

Jesus cried unashamedly. In Hebrews 5 v 7 it is recorded *"during the days of Jesus' life on earth, he offered up prayers and petitions with loud cries and tears to the one who could save him from death, and he was heard because of his reverent submission."*

Paul the Apostle could say *"I serve the Lord with great humility and with tears"* (Acts 20 v 19).

I have no doubt in my mind about the validity of such expressions of feeling and Grace and I are both grateful to God that we have been privileged to see this happen with such amazing regularity. We are confident that the Lord is using this ministry at this particular period to do a special work in people's lives. We continue with the assurance of the words in Psalm 126 v 6 firmly established in our hearts: *"Those who sow with tears will reap with songs of joy. He who goes out weeping, carrying seed to sow, will return with songs of joy, carrying sheaves with him."*

Chapter 6
Awakening Dreams

I sat watching Martin Luther King on the television. He was addressing a crowd of thousands at the Lincoln Memorial, who had come to hear him share his thoughts and vision for a world where black people were treated equally and where black and white could live together in harmony. As the man spoke out of the depth of his feelings, the atmosphere became electric and was discernible even through the television set. Every word he spoke was like dynamite and I could not help but be caught up in the emotion of the moment. Time and time again he repeated a phrase which seemed to express all the longings of the thousands of people assembled. "I have a dream," he declared, and each time he said it he went on to explain what his dream was.

"I have a dream" he cried, and those around him on the platform could be heard to mutter agreement.

"I have a dream" he repeated, and you could feel the vast crowd responding.

"I have a dream," he emphasised again, and as those words took hold of me, so I found myself leaping up out of my chair, punching the air with my fists, shouting "so have I, so have I!"

In that moment something happened to me. I saw that impossible dreams could become reality. If God was the God of the impossible, why could he not be so in the area of dreams. The things that I longed to see happen, were they merely the product of a very vivid imagination, or did God want me in fact to imagine them?

As a result I began to look at all the 'impossible' dreams in my life and ask God if He put them there, and whether He wanted to help me make them reality. Over a period of time I became convinced that God does want us to dream and see our dreams fulfilled and it is actually possible for Him to achieve the apparently impossible.

My mother's experience with regard to her vision of the Mission and my own of Ghana left me in no doubt about the matter, and before too long I started to minister along the lines of "Dreams and Visions", encouraging people to revive their dreams, or dream new dreams. It dawned on me that there were large areas in people's lives where they were extremely intense, and the will of God was one of the principle areas of problem. If you asked people "what is the will of God for your life?", great furrows appeared on their forehead and the intensity began to creep in, because they often seemed unable to identify it clearly. Far from being good, perfect and acceptable, the will of God for so many seemed to be good, perfect but totally unacceptable, and something that had to be submitted to with clenched teeth and iron resolve.

So many people live believing a lie. As a result of some sort of convoluted thinking and erroneous teaching, they have come to believe that what they want cannot be the will of God. The Lord, apparently, always wants something different to us. Our thoughts are simply not to be trusted. It would also seem to be the case that if you enjoy doing something, it could not possibly be God's will for you. His will is not to be enjoyed, perish the thought! What an awful travesty of the truth!

As I ministered to people, I realised that they needed to be asked a different question. Instead of asking, "what is the will of God for you?", I asked, "have you got a dream?" Immediately there was a response, and in a relaxed way people were able to tell me all the things that they had cherished in their hearts: places they wanted to go, things they wanted to do. They could easily imagine themselves doing certain things, but because they were not sure it was the will of God, did not dare to pursue their dreams. They had become accustomed to seeing the will of God like a tightrope along which you have to balance very carefully, for if you make one false step, all will be lost.

"Couldn't what you are dreaming about be what God wants you to do?" I encouraged them.

"But it seems so fanciful" they would often reply.

"That's all right" I said "God is in the business of being fanciful. He has given you your imagination to use and more often than not He wants to use what is in your imagination."

We spend so much time worrying about the sort of things we should not let our imagination run away with, we do not give enough time for the Holy Spirit to plant seed thoughts in our minds, developing those thoughts through our imagination.

The more I have spoken to people along these lines, the more I have come to realise that if only half of the dreams in Christians' hearts were fulfilled, we could have revolutionised the world for Jesus Christ years ago.

Of Jesus it was written prophetically in the Psalms that he would delight to do the will of His Father. It gave Him great joy to be able to do those things that were pleasing to God and I am sure that He never regarded it as a narrow pathway where there is no room for choice. I feel there is confusion between the narrow way that Jesus referred to as leading to salvation, and the will of God for the Christian. We have made the will of God a narrow pathway, when often it is a broad meadow for us to enjoy and stretch our legs in, and it is no wonder that very few of us seem able to discover God's will for our lives, when we have accepted a warped version of the truth.

On a number of occasions in the Gospels we find sick people crying out to Jesus to be healed. Never is the son of God caught in a quandary about whether it is the will of God for Him to heal the person concerned. Never do we read that he asks the person, "are you sure that it is God's will for you to be healed?" Usually if He does ask questions, it is, "what do you want me to do for you?", and that is the question, I believe, that many people need to hear the Lord asking them with regard to their dreams and desires.

In Luke Chapter 2 there is a lovely story told about a man called Simeon and a woman named Anna. The baby Jesus was being brought to the Temple by his parents to be consecrated to the Lord, according to the Law and Jewish custom. As Mary and Joseph entered the Temple Courts an old man approached them. Simeon was clearly a man who was in touch with God, for we read that at some point in his life it had been revealed to him that he would see the Christ of God before he died. We are not told how long it was before Jesus was born, but the passage seems to suggest that it was some time, perhaps a number of years prior to the event.

Simeon had a dream. Like all devout Jewish people, he longed to see the Messiah, the one who would bring peace to the land and establish a rule of righteousness and justice. Unlike most other people, however, he had been given the assurance that he would see the anointed one of God in his lifetime. I wonder if he shared that knowledge with other people or kept it to himself? When he first received the revelation it must have felt almost too hot to handle. For centuries his people had talked about "when the Messiah comes", and suddenly the day of his appearing was within Simeon's grasp. Everything within him must have wanted to shout it from the roof-tops.

He held the word in his heart and dreamt. Time went by and still Simeon waited. The initial excitement of the revelation wore off a little in the continual round of work and mundane events of life, but underneath all of this, the old man still believed he had heard from God.

One day he felt compelled by the Spirit of God to go out into the Temple courts. As he obeyed and entered the court area he saw a young couple carrying a baby. At that moment it was as though a light went on in his mind. "This is the one you have been waiting for!"

Hardly able to contain his excitement, he moved as quickly as he could towards the young couple. He stopped them, muttered a few words of introduction and then said these lovely, prophetic words:

"Sovereign Lord, as you have promised, you now dismiss your servant in peace. For my eyes have seen your salvation, which you have prepared in the sight of all people, a light for revelation to the Gentiles and for glory to your people Israel." (Luke 2: 29-32).

In a few brief moments Simeon's dream had been awakened and become reality. He knew now that he could leave this life in peace. God had fulfilled his word to him.

Mary and Joseph simply were amazed at what Simeon had said, but if there was any doubt in their minds, it would certainly have been dealt a severe blow by what happened next.

Anna was an old woman of 84. Her husband had died only seven years after they had married, and she had given herself to worshipping God night and day in the Temple, fasting and praying ever since. What a woman, how she must have loved God. Undoubtedly she too was looking for the Messiah, for the Bible calls her a prophetess and she was, therefore, well aware of all the scriptures foretelling His coming.

At the same moment as Simeon was finishing what he had to say, she too came over to Mary and Joseph, gave thanks to God and began to tell other people about the child Jesus to all who were looking forward to the redemption of Jerusalem. Her dreams had come alive too!

What a thrill it is when this happens. What a joy it is to belong to a God who delights in making dreams come true. As I move around the country and abroad in different church situations, I realise that there are so many people who have held dreams in their hearts for many years. Some have grown discouraged because their dreams have failed to become reality as quickly as they would have liked. Others have found their lives overtaken by all the demands that family, home, work and yes, even church demand of us, and their dreams have faded. Inevitably there are those who feel their dreams have been shattered by some traumatic or dramatic experiences in life, and every hope they had lies in pieces around their feet.

To all these people I am able to say with utter confidence, "God is in the business of restoring and mending broken dreams and fulfilling our heart's desires. He makes that which seemed at times to be no more than a pipe dream, a living reality."

Wherever I go and speak on this subject I always encourage families to get together in the meeting. I feel deeply concerned about the dreams parents have for their children, but never express them. In an effort not to force their children into a mould, many parents fail to tell their children about the desires they have for them, which could well be exactly the sort of guidance they need when they are considering their future and what they can contribute in life.

On the other hand, there are a number of people who have allowed society to dictate the sort of roles their children are going to play. The world view is that material security is of utmost importance, and constantly bombarded by this message, many Christian parents start to think along the same lines. Instead of asking "what does God want my child to do?", they see the important things as a good, secure, well-paid job; a good pension; a nice house with all the necessary modern appliances and a little bit of money in the bank for a rainy day. Where does the Kingdom of God fit into all this? Where are those who will dream of their sons and daughters being missionaries, evangelists or pastors? I know that if I had a son I would want him to be a preacher and I am praying that Simon Barnes Norton will be just that.

I am convinced that there are parents who have aspirations for their children, but cannot believe that God is good enough and big-hearted enough to make their hopes reality.

I always encourage them to pray for their children, to speak out to them what is in their heart for them; what they long to see happen in their lives; to prophesy specific things to them about themselves and to pronounce blessings on them. If it is possible to unwittingly curse our children by the negative things we say, it must be possible to bless them and bring something positive about in their lives.

I particularly encourage parents to pray for their children when they are asleep. There is something strangely intimate about a child's bedroom when they are in bed and sound asleep. The child is completely relaxed and whatever he or she may have done during the day, there is a sort of innocence about them as they lie in blissful slumber. It can be a very moving time, just to stand in the semi-darkness and watch your child for a while and I know many parents who feel like that and can identify with the sense of intimacy I am talking about.

I wonder how many have, in those special moments, poured out their hearts to God for their children. How many have longed for the Spirit of God to rest on them and prayed that Jesus would use them for His eternal purposes and glory. It is an opportunity that all parents should take hold of in order to see their dreams and aspirations worked out for their children.

Children should be encouraged to dream their dreams for God. In their simplicity and child-like faith they can often be more easily in tune with the heartbeat of the Holy Spirit than the adults. I believe every child of Christian parents should have a world map in their bedroom to study, pore over, and be able to ask God "what part do you want me to play in this world for you? The earth is yours, is there anywhere you want me to go? What contribution can I make?"

The young son of a friend of ours did just that and came to his daddy and said, "I feel God wants me to go to South America."

With a wry smile on his face, dad replied, "well son,

South America is a big place. I think you will have to be more specific.'' The boy went away and for a few days prayed about the matter. He returned to his dad to announce three specific countries to which he felt he should be going.

It would be all too easy to be patronising on these occasions and fob our children off with an "O.K. we'll see what happens"' type of answer. But this dad did not do that. He believes his young son is capable of hearing God and consequently he is making plans to visit at least one of those countries with his son in the next year or two. That is what you call pursuing dreams!

When I have families together in meetings in the way that I have described, I get the husband and wife to face each other. I first ask them to lay hands on each other, (not cuddle each other, there are plenty of other opportunities for that!), and then I ask the wife to prophesy to her husband and speak out all the things that she longs to see happen in his life. For wives this is not too difficult, for I usually find they are very aware of their husband's desires and longings for God. Then I ask the husband's to do the same for the wives. As much as I hate to admit it, husbands are not always so aware of their wives' dreams. Dare I say that the men can be a little selfish in pursuit of their own goals in life, expecting wives to trail along happily behind?

In these moments when husband and wife are facing each other and speaking out what they believe to be true for each other, all sorts of promises come to light that people received when they were first converted, or got married for example. Things are unlocked in their lives and begin to be released so that they start to become a blessing to the body of Christ. Their dreams and aspirations are awakened and begin to come to pass.

How exciting it is to see this happen and what a relief for so many people to find that the will of God is very much in line with what they had wanted to do any way. Their desires were God's desires and they begin to see the truth of those words of scripture, *"Delight yourself in the Lord and He will give you the desires of your heart. Commit your way to the Lord, trust in Him and He will do this."* (Psalm 37 : 4 & 5)

Tap, Tap, Tap

I have already mentioned about Olive Peter's desire to go to India as a young lady, and how subsequently in her 60's she eventually got there with Ernie, her husband, to help out at the orphanage run by Jochen Tewes.

Olive, however, cherished another dream. It was not what you could call a big dream, or even an impossible dream. It was nearer to an improbable dream. For most of her Christian life she had moved in circles where dancing was frowned upon and regarded as worldly and sinful. It was certainly no different at the Mission for a number of years.

One day she came to see me and told me that ever since she had been a young girl she had really longed to be able to tap-dance. Her age had not blunted that desire in any way. I felt simply "why not?" and encouraged her to go to tap-dance lessons.

She needed no further urging and enrolled herself on a beginners course. This meant that she was learning beside people very much younger than herself, but Olive was not deterred by this and persevered. Not only did she learn to tap-dance, she learnt well and went on to reach professional standard.

Now, in our meetings, when worship is flowing and people are dancing to the Lord, just occasionally Olive will put on her tap shoes and you can hear the tap, tap, tap as she dances before the Lord who has given her the ability to express her joy and feelings in this particular way.

Let us never limit God to what he wants to do for us. We can become so spiritual in our approach to life, that we miss out on the simple pleasures he wants us to enjoy. He has made us creative beings, because we are made in the image of the creator and it is, therefore, no wonder that we find ourselves longing to achieve things in this realm. There is no desire in our heart too unimportant for our loving heavenly Father; no dream too small that he would not love to see us bring to fulfilment.

Waltzing Around

A woman called Joyce came to see me and said, "I don't understand this Norman, but as I was praying I saw a vision of you and Grace waltzing around the main hall at the Mission."

In those days we were certainly not into ballroom dancing of any kind. "Well Joyce", I replied, "I don't know how that is going to come about, but let's just put it on the shelf and wait and see what happens".

Some period of time after that, Christine Jaques, one of the young women in the fellowship, also came to see me, in tears. She loved ballroom dancing and had reached Gold Medal, or professional standard. Increasingly, however, she found the time involved was cutting across her involvement with the Church and after a great deal of struggle she knew she had to make a decision. It was heart-breaking for her.

"I know what I've got to do" she said through the tears, "but it is so difficult."

I prayed with her and then tried to encourage her. "I don't understand it either Christine, but I know what you have to do is right. If you will hold it in your heart, God will somehow, in some way, use what you give to him. I don't believe he has put it in your heart for nothing. Just give yourself to dancing for God, it may not be the same, but do it anyway." Which is exactly what she did, and in our times of worship she would dance before the Lord in a way that blessed God and us. She was, in fact, very good at interpretative dance, even though she did not particularly feel it herself.

We were slowly, as a group of people, loosing ourselves from the bonds of legalism. We had been through a period where, as Christians, we felt it would be totally out of order for us to go to parties of any description. But as we began to enjoy the grace of God, so we realised that we could actually attend certain functions such as the office party, without sinning. We had only one problem. None of us had a clue as to how to dance. We could not put one foot in front of the other without tripping over it. We were like a bunch of wallflowers.

I began to pray about the situation, feeling that something should be done. All of a sudden an idea hit me. I went to see Christine Jaques.

"Christine I've got a proposal for you" I said. "Would you be prepared to run Saturday morning ballroom lessons for members who are interested? If you want, you can even charge for what you do."

Christine nearly fell off her seat. "I can't believe it" she replied, " a month ago I was moaning to the Lord about having to do all this interpretative dance. I asked him if there was any way I could do ballroom dancing and teach other people what I know. Now you come with this. Of course, I'd be delighted!"

Consequently a series of lessons were started at the Mission on Saturday mornings. The first lesson was "How to do a Waltz." I took my wife and waltzed around the main hall of the Mission. The exact fulfilment of the vision seen by Joyce two years previously. That is how God works!

It does not matter how ridiculous our dreams might seem. If we share them, speak them out, there is every possibility that the words we speak will become flesh.

I have used these two examples to show that God can take what might seem fairly insignificant dreams and make them reality. There are scores of other people who have experienced similar things and who know that he is a God who is interested in every aspect of our lives and wants to see us fulfilled in every area of our being. He knows just how important things are to us as individuals, and because of this they are important to him. Providing they will not hurt our character or lead us astray in any way, I believe he will do all in his power to awaken our dreams and help us to pursue them until we see them become reality.

Chapter 7
India - Frustration and Fascination

After two hours of being shunted back and forth between different enquiry desks, I was getting nowhere and certainly becoming more than a little frustrated by Delhi Airport. I was beginning to wonder if I should ever have applied to the Shaftesbury Society for the £1500 grant they were offering to a leader who had served over seven years, in order to take a three month sabbatical to travel. The one thing every person dreads who travels by plane had happened to me. I had lost a piece of luggage.

My experiences of Ghana had taught me that only the English queue. Once we arrived in the airport terminal at Delhi it was a mad rush for the luggage carousels. Everybody pushed and shoved everyone else, regardless of age or sex. Four Jumbo Jets had arrived at the same time. The luggage of around 1200 people was cascading down onto the carousels, and nobody knew what carousel their particular pieces of luggage were on. It was absolute madness! All around was a twenty foot high pile of uncollected luggage, and people were jumping over carousels, going back and forth, trying to find their suitcases.

I had already spotted Ian Farr, my long time friend from Yeovil, waiting for me. He was probably used to such scenes, having been in India for some years. I waited at the carousel for over an hour, and still only two of my three pieces of luggage had turned up.

I went to the first enquiry desk and after waiting some time for attention, was politely guided towards the British

119

Airways desk. Here there was another solid bank of luggage 150 feet long, 10 feet wide and 6 feet high. Once again I waited some time at the desk, but eventually got some service. I explained my predicament, was offered forms to fill in, and shown a sheet of paper with pictures of various kinds of suitcases to try and identify what my case looked like. The problem was mine looked like none of them. I pointed at one which was vaguely similar and was told to return the next day. The next day, however, I would be a further plane ride away, hopefully enjoying the hospitality of the Farr family in Mussoorie. I consoled myself with the thought I would be returning to Delhi for a visit in one week's time and could hopefully collect the missing case which contained all my presents for the people I would be visiting.

Eventually I was able to leave the airport and so headed for the Customs Hall. As I entered the area I was stopped and asked if I had a Customs Declaration form. Of course, I had not! Once again, very politely, I was told I must have such a form, filled out in triplicate before I could pass through Customs. I went to the appropriate desk and queued to get attention. The official seemed very reluctant to hand over the form, and then the penny dropped. Or should I say the rupee! The reason why I had experienced so many problems and so much delay was that I wan not paying anybody money to speed things up. By this time I was tired, frustrated, hot and very angry. I looked at the official and told him in no uncertain terms that there was no way I was going to pay him and insisted that he gave me the form that I needed. With the smile still intact on his face and his politeness seemingly unruffled, he handed it over immediately.

After three hours I was more than relieved to meet Ian Farr and leave the airport. We were due to spend a night at the house of a local pastor and so jumped in a taxi. As we drove from the airport, the incredible contrasts of India began to hit me. One moment a Mercedes flashes by, the next vehicle could well be a rickshaw or a camel cart. I was struck by the sheer weight of numbers of people and thousands of them seemed to be riding bicycles.

There were Hindu shrines on every street corner and in every taxi. The temples ranged in size from an ant hill to buildings over 100 feet tall. Cows wandered around the High Streets and of course, if you hit one of these animals, you get out and run for your life!

It was very easy to compare India with Ghana. There was more food in the shops in India, yet somehow the people looked poorer. For every one unkempt person you would have seen in Ghana, I saw hundreds more in India, almost certainly because of the vast population, a staggering 700,000,000 people at the time of my visit.

We stayed the night in a pastor's house, and returned to the airport next day to fly north to a place called Dehra Dun airport, which is basically a tarmacadam strip in the middle of nowhere. The airport buildings were actually tents! Security was very tight because of the tension between the Sikhs and Hindus, and our luggage was thoroughly searched, as were we. I even had to remove my shoes and socks and have the bottom of my feet inspected!

From the town of Dehra Dun we had to take a taxi ride of 60 kilometres in order to get to the Farr's home in Mussoorie. The journey was hair-raising to say the least. The only discipline on the road is size. If you drive a 40 ton truck, you are king of the road and everything else gets out of the way. The smaller your vehicle, the less important you are until you reach the pedestrians, who are definitely the lowest of the low.

Mussoorie is 7,500 feet above sea level and is situated in one of the most beautiful spots in India, the foothills of the Himalayas. It was not until I actually got into the Farrs' house, however, that I was able to appreciate the beauty of the surroundings. 7,500 feet is a long way up when your taxi driver is driving at full speed round hairpin bends, and a long way down when you are looking down the side of the mountain! Sight seeing is the last thing on your mind. Prayer is the number one occupation for the duration of most of the journey!

Once out of the taxi we had to walk further to Ian's house with our luggage, and I must admit, it felt like walking up ladders against a wall, so steep was the climb. We made it eventually, tired and weary, but glad to be at our destination. Now there was time to enjoy the scenery. The foothills in which Mussoorie lies would be regarded as huge mountains by most British people. The view from the Farrs' house was nothing short of breathtaking. As I gazed at the foothills becoming increasingly higher, finally leading to the Himalayas, I kept waiting for someone to turn the page. Everything was so still it was like a picture out of a book. I found it difficult, however, to cope with the fact that there was so much poverty in evidence all around me, set against the backcloth of these beautiful surroundings.

That afternoon we visited an orphanage in Mussoorie, run by an Indian couple called Swami and Pami. They presented me with a garland of flowers and then showed me around. I was easily moved to tears as I was shown the facilities available. In the West we would consider the beds they used fit only for burning! Each child had a tin plate and cup, but very few other possessions. By Indian standards they were fairly well dressed and cared for, and received a good education.

The Home was run down due to lack of funds. Swami and Pami were originally sponsored by a group of Christians in the West, but because the couple came into a charismatic experience, all financial support was cut off, leaving the orphanage stranded.

The following day we were invited by the couple to dinner. They had nothing, but gave us such a lovely meal (which I subsequently discovered was curried buffalo meat). After the meal I shared with them from the scripture, "such as I have, I give to you," encouraging them that they may not have had rupees, but they did have Jesus and could share him with others. We prayed for Swami and Pami and then encouraged the children to gather round them and bless their adopted mum and dad. Tears flowed easily for everyone, and I prophesied to Swami, particularly that he would learn to weep himself. I was told later that the things I had prophesied had apparently confirmed in minute detail things about which God had been speaking to him directly.

We met Swami and Pami the next day for lunch and discussed their situation at the orphanage. It was a very honest time, the result of which was that Ian Farr got involved to help in whatever way he could. As a result of that involvement, Links International gave a gift of £500 to the home, with the promise of a further £500 at a later date. How blessed I was that God had already opened up a way to serve and had not allowed me to go to that vast continent merely for sight-seeing.

Not for Shirts and Trousers

Two weeks before I departed for India, I was at a conference in Nottingham. While there I shared about my forthcoming trip. A man came up to me after I had spoken, saying that God had given him something to tell me. He said that I was not to go to India "for shirts and trousers", that is, the main emphasis was not going to be for relief work and the ministry of Links International. I was to go with the word of the Lord in my heart and be faithful to deliver it, speaking out with confidence what God had said.

For preachers, such words are a real encouragement but do not pose too much of a problem. We are used to speaking, and delivering the word of the Lord is a real joy, and what our job is all about. Little did I realise, however, quite what that would entail.

Woodstock is an international school, attended mainly by the children of Europeans and Americans working in India. Ian and Gwen Farr's children were both pupils. One evening we were invited to speak to a group of about 25 of the staff, all Christians. I spoke and felt very free at the end to move out and prophesy over different people. Again the prophecies were very direct, detailed and encouraging. All in all I spoke to about seven people in this way, who all ended up weeping but obviously blessed by God.

Almost a month later, still in India, but getting towards the end of my stay, I had a very unusual night. At about 3 a.m. I woke up and God spoke quite clearly to me about Woodstock School Christian Union, where I was to speak again on the following evening. He gave me prophetic words for the people which were so vivid, that in the morning they were still fresh in my mind without having written anything down. That was not all, however, the Lord also showed me little dramas, or props I was to use with each word, to make them more real. This was really putting the pressure on me. I had never done anything like that before and felt that I would really be going out on a limb. I could hardly cope with it, but determined to move out in faith, knowing that it would cost me everything.

I was in fear and trembling over the things God had revealed to me as we went to the school that evening. I spoke on my favourite theme of 'Dreams and Visions' and as I did so, once again the Spirit of God touched people's lives, causing them to weep, repent, be quickened and start to believe again some of the things the Lord had placed in their hearts. As fresh hope was rekindled, so ground was regained from the enemy.

Encouraged by the response up to that point I started to give the prophetic words that God had given to me at 3 a.m. that morning. The first person I spoke to was Ian Farr. I placed a blanket over his head and I am sure that Ian wondered what on earth was happening. "For a period of

124

time" I said, "you have been hidden, but the day of your appearing is near." Ian just burst into tears. Some period of time afterwards, I was to discover that this was the beginning of him being launched out into a much wider sphere of ministry in India, when he was able to capitalise on the contacts he had built up.

I went to one woman, held her hand and asked for the light to be turned out for a few seconds. "I am as embarrassed about this as you are" I said to everyone, "but God has told me to do these things. Please turn the light back on." I looked at the woman.

"Did you notice before the light went out I was holding your hand" I asked.

"Yes."

"Now that the light is on again, I am still holding your hand. God says that he will never leave you, even though you have felt darkness in your spirit. He will never let you go." She was clearly blessed by the word and reduced to tears.

I turned to another couple. "I see you with babies in your arms."

"Oh no" they replied, "we don't want any more." —

"No, God is going to bring to birth new things in and through you. A new day is dawning for you." I did not know at the time that they were leaving this school to start a new work.

To another couple I said, "I see a word over you. It is 'security'. There is a security about your relationship that blesses people. God wants you to teach others about marriage."

They looked genuinely astounded. "We can't see that we are any different from anyone else" they said. Everyone in the room burst out laughing, for it was so obvious that they had a good marriage but they had never seen it as exceptional.

Some of the people I had words for were not present, so

125

the next day I went round the campus looking for them. I went to the house of an American couple whom I had never met before. As I stood in one of their rooms with them, I asked everyone to hold hands and spoke to the couple. "The Lord wants you to know that you are part of the Body of Christ and not separated from everyone else. You have been more effective than you realise, for God has used you. By getting everyone to hold hands, the Lord simply wants to show you what friendship is all about."

I also found a New Zealander called Geoff. "The Lord has told me to wash your feet."

"No, no, I can't cope with that" he replied, refusing to let me do it. I just got on and did what the Lord had instructed me to do, taking a bowl of water and a towel, and washed his feet.

"The Lord wants to honour you in this way because you have so willingly laid down your life for others," I told him.

"I can't see how I have served" he replied.

"God's word for you Geoff is, I was hungry and you gave me something to eat, I was thirsty and you gave me something to drink, I was a stranger and you invited me in, I needed clothes and you clothed me, I was sick and you looked after me, I was in prison and you came to visit me."

"When have I done that?" he asked, genuinely astounded. He could not think when he had done anything like that. It was almost a replay of Jesus' words in Matthew 25. So I answered with the words of scripture.

"Whatever you did for one of the least of these brothers of mine, you did for me."

Even though Geoff found it difficult to accept that what he did was anything other than absolutely normal for Christians to do for one another, Ian Farr knew that he was the sort of person who opened up his home for just about everybody and failed to realise the depth of his serving and how much God appreciated it.

Having finally discharged all the words God had given to

me, I felt elated and satisfied. If I had come to India only to experience this, the trip would have been more than worthwhile, for there is nothing quite so exciting and rewarding as seeing God's words speak to people in their situations and provide answers, encouragement and hope.

Orphans, Orphans and more Orphans

Orphanages must be one of the major growth industries in India. What a tragedy!

Nothing is destined to touch the emotions more than the sight of a child that has lost its parents for one reason or another, and who looks disorientated, isolated, bewildered and drained of hope. Thank God for the many organisations seeking to provide a home, food and education for thousands of children in this condition in India.

Many parents are forced to leave their children at the doors of the orphanage because their economic situation is impossible and one more mouth to feed is just not worth thinking about. Imagine the despair these people must have been driven to, to have to carry out such a deed. They did not find it any easier to do than we in more affluent countries would. They do not feel good about it. They mourn the loss of such a child from their family life, but cruel circumstances drive them to such acts of desperation.

I have described the work that Swami and Pami were doing. A few days after my arrival in India, we were to visit another orphanage, in a place called Sailikui, a taxi and jeep ride away, which amounted to several hours more of hair-raising driving.

The contrasts of India were once again evident on the journey. One moment we were passing an ex Raj's palace in all its magnificence, and within a very short space of time, we saw huts, hovels and broken down tenements. We eventually arrived at our destination early evening, but in the dark, to the sound of baying hyenas.

The orphanage is based on 30 acres of land, although only 20 acres are useable due to the presence of squatters on the other 10. It is run by a young couple called Ken (Yip) and Frieda McRae with their two young children. They originally came to India as hippies, but were converted to Christ.

They started the orphanage for boys and at the time of my visit, the farm project was two years old. The house had no electricity, so we sat down by oil lamp and candles. Only a few rooms had windows and the family was very poor. Life is difficult and Yip and Frieda have lived sacrificially, only taking one break in 8 years of hard work.

There were 19 boys in care and their ages ranged from 12 to 18 years. Yip has learnt all his skills while carrying out the work himself and his vision is to teach and train the boys so that they can obtain work outside. This has already begun to happen and is a major feat in itself.

The farm was officially opened by the Canadian High Commission, who gave a generous grant towards the project. They were already farming wheat, rice and mangoes and had plans for future expansion, to include a citrus orchard, vegetable garden and livestock.

They had many problems to overcome, including the need of a good tractor.

Yip is a man of immense vision, who has more ideas than he will ever have time to fulfil, but I have nothing but admiration for both him and Frieda who have worked in very primitive conditions to see their dream fulfilled. I am convinced they will see it happen and was moved and blessed to be able to share in what they were doing.

In the south of India we met another man with a dream in his heart which is evidently being fulfilled. Jochen Tewes from Germany and his Indian wife Joshy lead the work of Inter-Mission in India. What they have achieved in quite a short space of time is amazing and it is clear that the hand of God is with them.

They are responsible for 68 orphanages in all, caring for 2,800 children. They are sponsored by donations from abroad, mainly from Germany, Holland, England and the U.S.A. The children are fed and clothed, given a home, education and free medical treatment, and when they are old enough, go on to the training schemes also being run by Inter-Mission.

As I looked at these children, it seemed to me that they were often far better off than a large number of other Indian children and are a real testimony to the work that is being done by the dedicated workers under Jochen Tewes, direction.

Around 60 boys attended a training school where they were taught carpentry or fitting and engineering. They were all orphans aged 15 to 20 years and by going through this training scheme will be able to obtain jobs outside of the work of Inter-Mission. Each one leaves the school with a set of tools if he is trained as a carpenter, or money if he is a fitter.

We also saw the girls training centre where there are 17 orphan girls who live in, and 20 more girls (described as being poor) who work on a daily basis. The girls are taught tailoring, and by doing so, are able to supply all the clothes for the Inter-Mission children, as well as bed-sheets and other necessary items. The school had already been helped by Tear Fund, but needed more commercial outlets in order to become self-financing.

There is a residential printing school which teaches 37 boys of 14 years old and upwards. The boys learn basic theory in a classroom situation and practical instruction on various types of printing machinery. At the time the project was rather weak due to the fact that the manager was about to retire, leaving a lack of direction and future planning. It was this particular opportunity that Links International took hold of, sending Ernie and Olive Peters out for six months, in order that Ernie could help to rectify some of the problems they were encountering, and Olive could have her dream of going to India fulfilled.

Nine Day Care Centres care for 50 children each. Mostly situated in slum areas, all the children receive food and milk free of charge and all the staff are paid by Inter-Mission.

Rather than build and establish their own churches, Inter-Mission supports 20 Indian churches and institutions, which includes other orphanages. This support for other establishments shows a creditable attitude and one that is a real example for many other organisations in India. This also involves supporting 200 pioneer workers at a cost of £10 per person per month.

There are also two farm projects, one of which is headed up by Yip and Frieda in north India. The other is on the site of one of the orphanages and when I visited it, was still only in its infancy.

We spent several days in Madras looking at all aspects of the work of Inter-Mission and I was impressed by the efficiency with which everything ran. The orphanages were excellent and the children were very well cared for and more than adequately equipped for life.

I was very challenged by the work Jochen Tewes was doing. He is a very self-effacing man whose leadership capabilities are beyond question. It was moving to meet a man who was prepared to leave the affluence of West Germany to pursue the dream God had put into his heart, and in so doing, to develop a work which is having an effect on so many lives that would otherwise be quite desolate.

The Dream-Like Continent

It does not take long to realise the power of Hinduism in India. Its grip is very powerful and evident in the number of shrines and temples you can see everywhere you go. It seemed to me that people's bodies and minds were brought under the control of this suppressive religion at all times, encouraged by the awful caste system that dictates your station in life. The fatalistic doctrine of Hinduism allows for no betterment in life. If you are a road-sweeper, you will always be a road-sweeper and your children will be road-sweepers too. You will never be able to change because that is your 'karma', your fate.

Communism will never succeed in India because Hindu culture will never allow for the poor to rise up in revolt against their lot.

I watched on different occasions with a mixture of anger at the enemy, and pity for the people whose minds have been so blinded as to worship trees, ant-hills and stone gods; who try to purify themselves by washing in pools of filthy water and who were locked into a dream-like existence of such hopelessness.

This is surely a real challenge to the Church. Most of the Christians I met had some sort of nominal Christian background before they were converted, and these were mainly in the south of India. There is very little evangelical witness in the north. Those who have been converted from Hinduism encounter a vast number of problems, mainly from their families. There are those who have been thrown out of their homes once they have professed faith in Christ, and have been totally cut off from their families. This would be a traumatic experience for anybody, but it is especially so for a Hindu, where the tightly-knit family plays such an important part.

Some parents will go to unbelievable lengths to persuade a Christian son or daughter to renounce their new faith,

131

sometimes resorting to bribery, and even arranging a marriage as a sort of trap. In some cases new converts who are under the age of majority, that is 18 years old, have to be almost secret believers if they are dependent on their parents.

I was told of one example where a whole Hindu family turned to Christ as a result of the quiet witness of one of the youngsters at home, but this event was almost unique and happens rarely in Hindu circles.

Ian and I spent two days with a man who has dared to challenge the might of Hinduism in no uncertain terms. Right down in the south-eastern corner of India is an island called Rameswaram which is the real centre of the Hindu religion. The whole island is, in fact, a Hindu shrine and the dream of every Hindu is to visit the place, its many shrines, bathe in the sea and wash in its 17 holy washing places. A diminutive man named Paulose felt God told him to go to Rameswaram to preach the Gospel.

In total obedience, Paulose moved with his wife and two children to the island, having nowhere to live, no money and unable to speak the language. He found two rooms for the family to live in, put his children into the school where they simply had to learn the language, and set about the task God had called him to do.

On our arrival on the island, I was immediately struck by the spiritual darkness of the place. It felt as if a cloud was permanently hanging over the island. The look on people's faces was one of utter despair. The whole island was given to temple worship with hundreds of shrines of all shapes and sizes. Some were no bigger than mounds of earth; others were huge, heavily carved stone buildings, intricately designed.

The extremes of poverty and wealth were all too clearly in evidence but accepted as part of the awful doctrine of karma. The inequalities of the caste system were also conspicuous, with beggars in abundance and the Bramin (high caste) strutting around displaying the evidence of their caste - a cord that hangs over their bare shoulders. Apparently they never remove this cord, even while washing.

In the midst of all this lived Paulose and his family. We were treated to a delicious meal in their humble home and shown real hospitality by this simple, but lovely family.

Paulose was originally trained by Operation Mobilisation, had a clear call from God and what I would term an apostolic ministry. At the time of my visit he had established a church of approximately 40 believers and another group of 30 believers in a nearby fishing village. He also had a group of 8 men whom he discipled on a daily basis, sending them out in evangelism. They suffer often for their faith, having been spat upon, beaten up and stoned. But still they go on. "We love Jesus" is the answer that Paulose gave when asked why he endured such opposition. I was continually moved by the things that I witnessed there.

The vision of the Church was to build a place to worship God on the island. When we arrived, the Lord had already given them a plot of land, which was quite miraculous considering the circumstances in which they lived, and I was left in no doubt they would see their vision fulfilled. Paulose, his family, and the growing Church were a real light in the middle of what is total darkness.

Bazaar Experiences

Because of the length of my visit to India (over one month), I was able to do a fair bit of normal sight-seeing, and the sights ranged from the amazing to the awful.

In Mussoorie I was able to visit a bazaar which I can only describe as fascinating. There was one main street with countless alleyways leading off it. Each alleyway was only 8 ft. wide, lined with tall buildings. Every shop was crowded with goods and equipment because space is at such a premium, in fact I saw one cubby-hole, about 3 ft. wide and 7 ft. high, divided in two horizontally, so that two men could work in it. One man worked on top with a sewing machine in a space 3 ft. by 3½ ft, and the other man below.

The smells of the bazaar hit you at every turn; curry, tea-brewing, cakes cooking, sweets and spices and a number of other smells I could not even identify. The range of different products and trades is amazing. I saw jewellers at work, engineers, cloth merchants, bakers, shoe-makers, iron-mongers, in fact, almost everything you could think of.

Bargaining is, of course, the fun part of any transaction in the bazaar. If you show interest in anything, the sellers always start with a high price. I learnt very quickly that, as a buyer, your answer to the first price quoted is always, ''what is the real price?'' and then the bargaining begins.

In a place called Ooty we visited the market. It was smaller and more compact than any of the other markets I had seen and therefore made quite a visual impact. It has specialised areas for each type of produce. There was a section for fruit and vegetables, all of which made an incredibly multi-coloured effect which must have taken hours to set up with the variety of goods on display. Then there was the jewellery with beautiful bangles, necklaces and ear-rings, and one lasting memory was of all the meat hanging on display - with millions of flies hanging onto the meat!

Of course, no visit to India would be complete without a visit to the Taj Mahal. It is a breath-taking, magnificent building, built as a mausoleum by one of the Muslim moguls for his wife. He planned to have another building of identical design built for himself in black marble, but died before the project could get properly underway and only the foundations are in.

I must confess that I thought it was one of the seven wonders of the world. It is not, of course, but ought to be! It is the sort of place you want to go back and see time and time again. As you walk into the archway, past the row of fountains, you see the classic view that is in all the pictures. The reflection of the building in the water in front is amazing. The whole place is a photographer's paradise.

It is built of shining white marble, in stark contrast to so much else in India. There are several optical illusions built into the place. For instance, there are pillars in front, which from a distance look hexagonal by design, but close up are, in fact, flat. The writing over the doorway creates another illusion. Standing underneath it, the writing ought to appear to get smaller to the eye the higher up the building you look, but it stays the same size all the way up. This is because the lettering has been slightly enlarged as it gets higher to create the illusion.

Inside, the place is dome-shaped. It is so designed that if you speak out loud, the sound of your voice will travel around for 15 seconds. Torches are shone onto the marble for visitors and such is the translucent quality of the marble, it appears as if the light is actually passing through it. It is difficult to find words to express the impression the building leaves on you, it is quite an experience. The shine was slightly tarnished for me, however, when I learnt that those involved in the building of the place were blinded and had their right hands cut off, so that such a marvel could never be re-created.

Right at the other end of the social scale, we were taken by James Roxborough of the New Life Fellowship in Bombay, to visit 'Slum City'. This is regarded as the worst slum in Asia. The smell was something I'd never experienced before, with refuse 2 ft. high everywhere, dirt, filth, poor drains, human excrement, sick dogs, dead cats, rats as big as cats, and millions of flies everywhere.

It was a city of huts of various shapes and sizes with alleyways three to four feet wide. One hut, 12 feet by 14 feet with no water or sanitation will cost between 25,000 to 30,000 rupees, which is about £2,000. A one bedroomed flat in Bombay costs £10,000 and the people earn a fraction of the average wage in the west.

Amidst it all, small businesses go on everywhere, even if it is only the business of sorting out rubbish. And right in the middle of all the filth and squalor stands a small church where 150 people cram in to worship the living God. A real testimony in the midst of all the Hinduism around them, they have already planted other churches elsewhere.

Sight-seeing in India is certainly a sight for the eyes and I found myself experiencing the full range of emotions at the various scenes I witnessed. A land of contrast is hardly the way to describe it!

While in the country, I was treated to the full range of food available. This is, of course, something tourists always worry about, afraid of suffering from the infamous Delhi Belly syndrome. I always found the hospitality over-whelming and no matter how poor the people were that we visited, we were treated to a sumptuous meal.

I ate everything from puffed wheat plus what appeared to be woodchip (!) in buffalo milk, through various rice dishes and onto a steak in the American Club in Delhi. Strangely enough, the only time I suffered from any stomach problems was after I had eaten English food.

One of my lasting memories to do with the food was on a trip from Mussoorie to Nainital. The taxi journey was eight hours long and as usual, pretty hair-raising (the customary wheel over the edge of the cliff stuff). We stopped at a little roadside place, you could not have called it a cafe, for refreshments. None of us had eaten breakfast so we were pretty hungry. I could see bread on display, and one look at the corners that had been nibbled by rats decided me firmly against any of that. Throughout the trip my policy had always been to play it safe with regard to food, so when I saw boiled eggs hanging up in wire baskets, I felt my safest course would be to have one of those. After all, it was in a shell, I could peel it myself, what could happen?

I did not bargain with the kindness of the gentleman who served me the egg. Instead of handing it to me in the shell, he proceeded to crack it and peel it with both hands. Boiled eggs are moist, and by the time he handed it to me, it was covered in dirty, sweaty, fingerprints. I then had to decide whether to eat the egg or go hungry. Having thought I would follow a policy of 'safety first', when it came to the crunch my policy went out of the window, or out with the shell anyway! I was so hungry, I said a quick prayer over the egg and ate it. Needless to say, I survived.

Assassination

My itinerary was interrupted by an event that hit the world's news headlines. We had flown from Bombay to Udaipur to meet a couple called Thomas and Mary Matthews, leading a church in the area. Mary leads teams of women in the surrounding villages, and at the time of our visit, had seen over 3,000 Indians baptised in 3 years.

As we were driving in a rickshaw, the driver told us of a rumour that Mrs. Indira Gandhi had been assassinated. The Russians, Americans and British had already broadcast the fact earlier in the day, but the Indian radio refused to announce her death in the afternoon, stating only that she was in hospital. This was a deliberate ploy on the part of the Indian Government. Because Mrs. Gandhi had been murdered by a Sikh, they knew there would be trouble, and so waited for people to be in their homes in the evening before any announcement was made. Once the news was made official, silence descended over the city and everything closed down for 24 hours.

Nobody quite knew what to do. We were far from home and Ian Farr had no idea what was happening in Mussoorie with his family, or they with him.

Everyone accepted that there would almost inevitably be tension and bloodshed, but no-one knew to what extent. All I wanted to do was to keep my head down and stay out of the way.

We did pray and take some authority over the situation. I remembered an occasion when there was bloodshed on the streets of Belfast and a group of people prayed that the Lord would bring peace to the area. As a result a sudden calm descended on the area whch was so significant as to be reported on the national news. Whereas the Christians around me in India simply accepted that there would be trouble, I felt that, as the people of God, we could speak peace to the nation and allow God to influence the situation. It turned out that we were in the quietest part of the country.

The next day, the 1st November, was mourning all day for Mrs. Gandhi and we could do very little as everything was closed down. On the 2nd November we got up at 6 a.m. to fly to Jaipur. At the airport there were very careful checks and quite a bit of tension, but eventually we were able to take off. We spent the day looking at the sights of Jaipur but by the evening the news told of some 400 people dead and curfew in many cities. On November 3rd Mrs. Gandhi's cremation took place. We waited with some degree of nervousness as the reports coming through were of some very dangerous situations with needless attacks on Sikhs and the obvious reprisals. A friend had seen the bodies of 12 people being loaded onto a lorry, Sikhs who had been decapitated. We were glad when this day was over.

The following day, a Sunday, we flew back to Delhi. Ian Farr felt very strongly that we should book and confirm our flight to Dehra Dun immediately, rather than wait for the next day when we were due to fly out. At the airport there were groups of Sikhs in huddles all around. At that point in time you never saw a Sikh alone; they stayed in groups for mutual protection and large numbers were in camps protected by the Army.

The tense atmosphere at the airport was tangible. I had never seen such a frightened group of people. Every time there was a loud noise, they virtually jumped out of their skin.

We prayed together about getting our flight confirmed, which is by no means a matter of course in India. Thankfully this was not a problem, but by the time we had made all the necessary arrangements, curfew had begun and we were not able to get a bus into the city to find accommodation for the night. The nearest hotel was the 5 star Centaur Hotel, and the only way to get there was by taxi, driven by a Sikh! I was very reluctant to take this course of action, but eventually my need for somewhere to sleep got the better of me, and I agreed. I spoke in tongues all the way to the hotel! The moment we went through the entrance doors, it was like stepping into another world; luxury is not the word. It was in such contrast to so much else just outside and I did not dare ask the cost. I simply booked the room and was glad of hot water to wash and a bed for the night.

How wise Ian had been to suggest confirming our flight. When we arrived back at the airport the next morning, the queue for seats seemed never ending. When we arrived in Dehra Dun, the evidence of trouble was plain for all to see, with buildings and houses burnt out. Here too, the atmosphere was tense. Needless to say, we were more than a little happy to be home in Mussoorie again. Although quietness prevailed when we arrived, there had clearly been some unpleasant moments. Taxis had been set light to and someone had been burnt alive. Ian Farr's children had been on a coach which was attacked and had all the windows smashed. They had laid all the Sikh children on the floor and tried to hide them. Another group from the school they attended had been forced to remain in a particular house in the town for five days while all around them property was being burnt to the ground. There had clearly been some very unpleasant moments in the preceding days. It was a relief, however, to find that no-one whom we knew had been injured in any way.

We waited in Mussoorie for things to calm down before continuing with our itinerary. Three days after our arrival home was a potentially dangerous time. The 8th November was the anniversary of the birth of Guru Nanak, the founder of the Sikh religion and the tension rose again as everyone waited to see what would happen. Thankfully, however, the day finished quietly with no major disturbances.

We were grateful to God for His protection over us during this very dangerous period and especially for the way the Holy Spirit seemed to lead us in safety in what were potentially hazardous situations.

Men of Vision

My experience of India had certainly broadened my outlook on life. I was challenged by many things that I saw and was grateful to God for the education that I was receiving on the trip, which was just one more step in the fulfilment of my own personal dream to touch the world for Christ. Nothing, however, quite challenged me as much as meeting people who clearly had a vision that had been given to them by God, and were in the process of seeing that worked out with obvious, positive results. I have already mentioned Jochen Tewes and the work he is doing with orphans. There were a number of others, all worth a mention, but I'll confine myself to just two works that left a lasting impression on me.

Our journey to Herbertpur was another of those memorable occasions! Indian drivers must have something of the spirit of the Gladiators in their blood. As we travelled in our jeep it was obvious, at times, that we were heading straight towards an oncoming truck. The game is not to get out of the way and see whose nerve lasts the longest! If we were not fighting over space with a lorry, we would be avoiding cattle, or cyclists who had spread themselves right across the road.

Other hazards included flash floods. These occurred in

the monsoon season. Often bridges were broken, and it was necessary to drive down into a dried out river bed and up the other side. With a sudden heavy downpour of rain, the river bed could be filled up with water in a very short space of time and it is not unknown for a coach, for example, to be crossing the river bed, a flash flood to occur, and the vehicle to be swept away. It is rather like a tidal wave. Thankfully we did not have this particular hazard to contend with on our journey.

We arrived at Herbertpur Christian Hospital where we were given delightful accommodation. Hot water came from a bucket with an element in it, but it was a treat to have electricity, a nice soak in a bath, be it only 3 feet long, pleasant convesation and a good sleep.

The hospital, founded by a Dr. Lehman, boasted 106 beds and 100 staff; 26 of whom were nurses. It is 75% self-supporting, the rest of the finance being provided by supportive bodies in the West. The medical superintendent, an American/Chinese by the name of Dr. Sy Satow, was a genuinely humble, gracious man who, of necessity, has to be a good all-rounder in the medical sense. One day he could be tackling major brain surgery, and the next a foot amputation. He is a caring man with a real love for God and people, and it was a privilege to spend several hours talking to him.

Paul East, now in Cyprus, was the hospital administrator. He took us on a tour of the hospital, which is designed in the shape of a quadrangle to simulate a village layout. This helps the people to feel at ease, and its unpretentious atmosphere further relieves patients of any strangeness or embarrassment that they might experience. When the weather is hot, or the hospital is overcrowded, the beds are put out into the square, under the trees, where it is cooler.

I was impressed by the simplicity of the place and moved by the evident needs. Nurses only supervise injections and the recording of the patients temperature; all other jobs are done by family and friends, even the cooking of meals. People come to the hospital from 50 to 60 miles from the east and west, and from as far away as 600 miles to the north. This means that there are a large number of hill tribe people and overall, a great mixture of cultures and backgrounds.

For 15 rupees (less than £1.00) per day, a patient can have a private room with inside water tap and cooking facilities. In addition, there are 4 de luxe rooms which have better kitchen facilities and tiled flooring at a cost of 20 rupees per day. There were certain conditions to be adhered to on admittance to the hospital, and these are clearly pointed out to the patients and their families. These are that the standard of care for each patient is the same, whether or not they occupy a private room; they cannot insist on a particular doctor or nurse to treat them; they cannot demand a particular bed or who they are beside in the ward. The latter two conditions can cause real problems when Hindus and Muslims are along side each other, and they also cut right across the caste system of Hinduism.

Our first stop was the outpatients department. Every patient is given a record card for which they pay 5 rupees and which becomes their property. In this way, no records are actually kept at the hospital itself. There are various examination rooms and one of the major problems at the time of our visit was the need of a female doctor for the Muslim women, who refuse to be examined by male staff.

People are treated first, then pay for the treatment afterwards. This helps those who may not be able to pay all the fees, for no-one is turned away through lack of money.

The wards, I would have to say, were in a pretty desperate state, although still fairly good by Indian standards. A British hospital would not cope with the number of people present at any one time, as relatives sit with the patients, feeding and caring for them. I was moved by the tragedy of some of the cases I saw; the twelve year old who had bone cancer, had had his foot amputated initially, then his leg to the knee, then thigh, now his hip needed attention. What hope was there for him? Then there was the man, a mason, who had lost both hands. How, I wondered, would he survive? So many looked hopeless. Thanks, however, to the dedication of men like Dr. Satow and his staff, many other patients recovered, grateful that there was a hospital where they could receive expert, caring attention.

Several of the wards were due for alterations and complete refits, but whatever is done, the battle against the sheer weight of numbers will always be an uphill struggle.

We visited the maternity ward, which had approximately 20 patients. It differed considerably from maternity units in the West. Indian mothers insist on having their babies in bed with them all the time, and although cots are provided, they are never used. In the ward was a premature baby, born at seven months into the pregnancy, seven days old and weighing only 2 kilos. No special care, it seemed, was provided. There were no incubators, which was a deliberate policy, as they can be dangerous pieces of equipment in the hands of the unskilled. Premature babies were wrapped in cotton wool, then in tinfoil, and left under a heat lamp. Babies who were jaundiced, were put under strip lighting and this, apparently, was very effective.

The delivery room, wash room and care areas were very good and it was obvious that the hospital was making real strides in these areas.

When we visited, a new theatre complex was being developed, and not before time! The old theatre had a low ceiling, cramped conditions, no proper recovery area, no ventilation. The atmosphere was something akin to that of a sauna! The new complex would soon start to make life a little easier for the surgeons, who had an incredibly busy schedule to cope with.

Another problem area in health in India is the increase of cases of tuberculosis which is now at epidemic proportions.

Herbertpur had 4000 T.B. patients on its books. To combat this the hospital had built a special T.B. unit in the grounds, the money having been provided by the Treasurer of Uttar Pradesh out of profits from the State Lottery, which must be used for charitable purposes.

The unit takes care of the chronically sick for three months and part of the care is a rehabilitation programme where trades are taught, as many can no longer continue with their former jobs. The biggest problem is educating the patients to carry on with the treatment, which must continue for 18 months otherwise it is ineffective and potentially dangerous. Dangerous because if the patient allows his programme of medication to lapse and treatment is required later, even stronger drugs have to be used which would be to his detriment.

Unfortunately T.B. is spreading at an alarming rate, easily transferable by coughing and spitting, two habits that are part of the Indian way of life!

Dr. Satow and Paul East are men with a vision; forward looking men who care for people and reveal the love of God in a very practical and needful way. They are not content to accept sub-standard conditions in the long term, although they will make do as an interim measure. Their lives and dedication were an inspiration and I was impressed by the fact that they had a 10 year plan for the hospital which was more than well on the way to being fulfilled.

A few weeks later on the trip I met two more men who have built a church of between 600/700 people, called New Life Fellowship situated in Bombay. Pastor Joseph, an Indian, and his co-worker James Roxborough, an Anglo-Indian, work together very well as a team and have been leaders of the fellowship since its beginnings.

The meetings were held in a Congregational Church in Bombay, which is filled to capacity. The fact that the fellowship had no building of its own was a real problem. They were trying to buy their own plot of land, but this involved a tremendous capital outlay.

We enjoyed the Sunday morning meeting that we attended, which was in English and Hindi. A lot of the songs were English songs that were being sung in many congregations in the U.K. and as a result, the fellowship plays host to many English speaking visitors who can participate in the meetings.

There is also a morning service for Tamil speaking people, and all in all, there are nine different meetings held for various groups of people.

This fellowship was probably one of the most progressive that I encountered while in India. It was quite a radical movement in the sense that they have approximately 15 house groups, each with its own leaders. Various groups in the U.K. have had input, but possibly have done some damage because they wanted to do a take-over bid, inferring that the Indians do not know how to run their own affairs. This has caused a lot of heartache and sorrow for the fellowship and consequently they have become a little wary of too much involvement from outside. I was, however, very impressed by the work that these two men have done, the obvious growth they have experienced and the way they have reached out and seen people saved and changed by the power of the Gospel, especially in Slum City. I left them with the hope that continued contact and a building of relationships over a period of time would help to heal some of the wounds of the past.

After lunch with the Roxborough family, we went for a walk on a nearby beach. This was an eye-opener for me and confirmed to me that India is up and coming! To look at the families on the beach, you could have been anywhere in the world. There were people (mainly Indian families) in carriages, on horse-back, having pony rides, enjoying the fun fair and buying food. These were, of course, the people with money. But the stark contrast between rich and poor is everywhere, even in Bombay. The modern hotels and blocks of flats stood proudly on the waterfront, shining examples of the luxury and wealth that is available to the few. In their shadows stood the straw huts in which the poor live.

I tried several times whilst in Bombay to telephone home. Each time I was unsuccessful and I did not even get the call out of the country. While visiting another group called Living Word Fellowship however, I booked a call to London and got through. Imagine my feelings as I heard the ringing tone in my own house. The 'phone rang, and rang, and rang. There was no one at home to answer and I could not have been more disappointed.

Whilst travelling on a train in Bombay, my heart sank as I read a poster which said "Abortions 70 rupees - 2 hours back to work". I was horrified to think that for less than £5 a human life could be extinguished with the promise that in two hours the woman concerned could be back at work as if nothing had happened. I learnt that when Sanjay Gandhi was alive, he enforced a programme of sterilization, that is, soldiers would surround a village and vasectomies would be performed on all the men. The result was that as soon as villagers heard news of soldiers approaching, the men would take themselves off to the foothills to hide, leaving only the women in the village. Contraception plays no major part in family life in India, hence the sad advertisement in the train.

Such is India, a land of incredible contrasts, multi-cultural, multi-faith, multi almost everything. There was certainly never a dull moment on my trip, and at the end of it I knew that God had enlarged my vision just that little bit more. I had seen and been moved by the utter poverty of so many and almost unthinkable living conditions; angered by

146

the grip the enemy seems to have over so many lives, but heartened and encouraged by the examples of men and women who have given sacrificially for the sake of Christ and people he died for. The needs of the country are so great, it would be almost impossible to even try and list them, but what a thrill it was to see Christians dedicated to helping solve some of the problems; Indians and those from other nations whose lives have become a real light in the darkness. My hope and prayer for India remains that the light will overcome the darkness, and the darkness will not be able to withstand it.

Home at Last!

I am so grateful to God for how he has opened up the way to my dream being fulfilled. I guess I am a bit of an adventurer at heart and I have no real problem with roughing it in different situations in other lands. I get excited about travelling abroad and enjoy all the new sights and experiences, as well as seeing opportunities to serve God and His people. No matter how much I travel, however, I am never sorry to come home, to my wife and to the people in my own fellowship.

Such were my feelings at the end of my trip around India. My life had been enriched and challenged, but as the time drew near to come home, I felt the anticipation in me rising.

My last experience of India was a game of Pool in the American Club in Delhi. For me it was an ideal way to end my itinerary and then it was off to the airport - destination London!

As I came into the arrivals foyer at Heathrow Airport I was greeted by 30 of my fellowship who got up at 5.00 a.m. to meet me. There were loud cheers, clapping, hugs and kisses all round. One onlooker commented, "my, that man does have a large family." How true, how grateful I was for such a caring community of people. While I was away on the trip they had faithfully prayed for me. I learnt that after my departure for India they were very concerned about my safety and welfare and prayed that God would keep a hedge around me to protect me. God spoke quite clearly to Olive Peters and said, ''It's not a hedge I've put around him, but a wall, nothing can get through that wall.''

Sometime later they were praying for me and asked God to make the wall even higher because they felt the enemy was trying to break it down. It was after this that they heard the news of Mrs. Gandhi's assassination and the subsequent unrest, and were able to relax in the fact that God had prepared them for this and that He was in control of the situation.

How good it is to have people around you who are willing to support you in your vision and ministry and help you to make your dreams come true by encouragement, service and prayer. Without the fellowship at home, I know that my own ministry would have very little validity. How gracious of God to make me wait and learn by building a fellowship in the way we have done.

I came home from India convinced that it would not be my last trip to that great continent, and so it proved to be. I returned with John Norton and his 10 year old daughter Victoria. (She, by the way, prayed all the money in for her fare to India). We visited Ernie and Olive Peters who were well into their 6 month stay in Madras at the printing works of Jochen Tewes, to encourage them and also to treat them to a short holiday. I was also able to renew some of my previous contacts and strengthen relationships further.

Our involvement with India has not finished. Although it is becoming more and more difficult for Europeans to stay in India, we can still visit and Grace has a dream in her heart to lead teams of women to various countries, to work particularly amongst the women. One of the countries is India, and we are praying and waiting on God about this project. We are confident that the God who delights to fulfil our dreams, as we delight ourselves in Him, will, at the right time, bring the teams together and open the doors for Grace to do what she feels the Holy Spirit envisioned her to accomplish.

Chapter 8
In Abraham's Footsteps

I have already looked at some examples from the life of Abraham. He is, of course, one of the heroes of the faith, a man who stands out as a giant in the pages of scripture. When God told Abraham to do something, it was done. He obeyed the voice of the Lord, even though what he had been asked to do seemed mystifying at times, very difficult on other occasions, and almost unreasonable in one or two situations. He had faith in God who had called him and he pursued the dream in his heart; the dream of a great nation and a land to dwell in.

Scripture, however, true to form, does not hide Abraham's weaknesses and mistakes. Undoubtedly we wish to follow in Abraham's footsteps in terms of his faith and faithfulness, but there are one or two areas of his life where it would be better simply to look at the footprints in the sand and learn from his mistakes.

He and Sarah had been told by the Lord that they would have their own son, even at their time of life. It seemed impossible. Time went by and Sarah did not conceive, but God had promised a son, and this was the only way he could fulfil his original promise of Abraham being the father of a mighty nation. The longer they waited, the more restless Sarah became. She was a woman affected, quite naturally, by the culture in which she lived, and at some point that cultural upbringing became a stronger influence on her than the promise of God. In Genesis 16 v 2 we find her at the end of her patience, and in her frustration she says to Abraham, *"the Lord has kept me from having children. Go, sleep with my maidservant; perhaps I can build a family through her."*

We know what the result of that union between Abraham and Hagar was - Ishmael. Instead of fulfilling all Abraham and Sarah's desires, the unfortunate child, even while still in the womb, became a bone of contention between Sarah and Hagar. Historically the descendants of Ishmael and Isaac fulfilled the word of God concerning Ishmael in verse 12 of the same chapter - *"he will be a wild donkey of a man, his hand will be against everyone, and everyone's hand against him, and he will live in hostility towards all his brothers."*

How easy it is to produce Ishmael! God speaks to us and we become excited at the thought of what he has said. We walk on air for a few days, our hearts apparently full of faith. We dream of seeing the word fulfilled. Time goes by and the initial excitement wears off. The voice that we heard so clearly may seem to have quietened just a little, and the excitement we felt has dulled. We become frustrated and impatient. God did say it - didn't He? Of course He did, then why is nothing happening? And before too long we find ourselves trying to give God a hand; engineering situations and circumstances to bring about what we long to see happen. Someone once said, "God has more problems with those who want to help him than he has with backsliders."

There is a difference between pursuing a dream in the sense of praying about it, walking through the doors that God opens, and taking the opportunities that He presents, and trying to fulfil the dream ourselves. Ishmaels will cause us nothing but frustration and heartache. If God has spoken, He will perform it and we can confidently leave it in His hands.

One of my favourite television programmes when I have the chance to watch it, is 'One man and his dog'. It is a competition between shepherds, and the object is to see which one can control his dog the best and get the faithful hound to herd the sheep around a course, fulfilling certain criteria along the way. It is amazing to watch the relationship and sense of communication there is between shepherd and his servant, the dog. A certain tone of voice, a special whistle, and the dog reacts, knowing exactly what to do. The sounds the shepherd makes are totally unintelligible to the untrained ear, but the dog hears and understands.

How different that is to the picture of the average dog owner and his faithful companion. So often you see Rover taking his master for a walk, straining at the leash, dragging his owner along, who is bravely shouting "heel, heel!" with absolutely no response. Once Rover is let off the leash, he charges off like a mad thing disturbing little children playing games, and getting involved in fracas with other dogs. His master shouts and bellows, but Rover is oblivious and only when the leash is placed round his neck, he is yanked firmly away and given a good scolding, does he reluctantly begin to obey.

It is so much like life with our Master, the great Shepherd. If we remain sensitive to his commands, wait for the slightest sound of his voice and respond, by so doing we will find that he can actually see the situation far better than us and the job gets done much more easily and quickly. Alternatively we can continue to pull at the leash, or even charge on ahead and find we end up in all sorts of trouble. Pursue your dream, but do not run ahead of God!

If we can learn what not to do from this incident in Abraham's life, there is another occasion recorded when we would most definitely want to emulate him, if not literally, then figuratively. By the time we get to Genesis 22 in our Bibles, Isaac has been around for a while. God's promise has been fulfilled. Abraham had his heart's desire, a son by Sarah. Things are looking good for the family. Then God speaks and we read these words in verse 2 as spoken to Abraham "*take your son, your only son Isaac, whom you love, and go to the region of Moriah. Sacrifice him there as a burnt offering on one of the mountains I will tell you about.*"

Abraham's emotional reaction is not recorded. God has certainly seemed to lay it on thick, reminding him that Isaac was his only son, the one he loved. Abraham was used to children being sacrificed to other gods. Did this mean that Yahweh was no different in this respect? Had he really heard aright? The Lord had promised Isaac, now he wanted to remove him from the scene. All of his dreams were embodied in this one life.

Scripture records that Abraham got up the next morning and did as he was told. It all sounds very matter of fact, yet I doubt if it was as easy as that. I can't imagine that he slept very much, if at all, that night. He must have wrestled with his conflicting thoughts and emotions all through the lonely hours. But he got to the place where he wanted to obey. What we have to remember, of course, is that Abraham did not know the end of the story. As far as he was concerned, God had requested his son's life and the only possible way that God could keep his promise to him was to raise Isaac from the dead, for as we read in Hebrews 11 v 19,

"Abraham reasoned that God could raise the dead, and figuratively speaking, he did receive Isaac back from death."

Abraham binds his son Isaac and lays him on the altar he has prepared. As he takes out the knife and is about to plunge it into the body of his beloved son, the angel of the Lord stops him. But he was prepared to do it, to lose his son and everything he hoped for. God was more important to him than anything else.

In all of our talk about dreams and visions it is vital to remember one thing, the Lord is more important than any dream, no matter how big or incredible it might be. We must always be in the place where we are prepared to let our dreams die if God asks it of us. Grace and I had to learn that very hard lesson with regard to a family of our own, and so many people have been brought to a similar place by God. What do we desire more? To see our dreams fulfilled or be obedient to God when it might seem that what he is asking of

153

us is totally contrary to what we felt he had at first placed in our hearts.

It is possible to pursue something so hard, desire something so much, that when we achieve it, or receive it, it actually dies on us. Something that starts off being sweet in our mouths can end up as very bitter in our stomachs. Our dreams may well be totally in line with what God wants for us, but if they become more important to us than God himself, in effect they become idols, and the Lord will test us in the same way he tested Abraham.

Abraham passed the test and was blessed to hear the words, *"now I know that you fear God, because you have not withheld me your son, your only son."* May we also hear those words concerning our desires and dreams.

The angel of the Lord continues and speaks a second time to Abraham. In verse 16 we read, *"I swear by myself, declares the Lord, that because you have done this and have not withheld your son, your only son, I will surely bless you and make your descendants as numerous as the stars in the sky and the sand on the sea shore. Your descendants will take possession of the cities of their enemies, and through your offspring all nations on earth will be blessed, because you have obeyed me."*

Abraham was prepared to let his dream die and obey God. As a result, God restored his dream and reaffirms his desire to do what he had originally promised. Abraham had learnt the principle of letting a seed fall into the ground in order that it might grow and bear fruit. May God give us the grace to do the same with the important things in our lives, for I believe in so doing we will find the Lord doing for us what he did for Abraham, and restoring the very things, precious hopes and dreams, that we were prepared to let die.

"I tell you the truth, unless an ear of wheat falls to the grounds and dies, it remains only a single seed, but if it dies, it produces many seeds. The man who loves his life will lose

154

it, while the man who hates his life in this world will keep it for eternal life'' (John 12:24, 25).

Chapter 9
Go East Young Man!

There are many different ways to receive guidance from God and many sermons have been preached on the subject, and not a few tracts and books written about it. I have found that when it comes to hearing from the Lord about a certain direction I should be taking, he often confirms what I feel he is saying through other people, usually by three or four people all saying a similar thing, although they may not even know each other, and may live hundreds, or even thousands of miles apart.

I mentioned in a previous chapter that while I was in Arkansas on a Retreat with a small number of leaders, one of those present told me that he felt I would, one day, visit mainland China. At the time I could not see how this would be possible, since I had no contacts at all in China, or knew of anyone who was involved in the country. But I accepted the word as from God and held it in my heart.

As I read about China I became more and more stirred about that vast land. I read all about the exploits of the missionaries, how they had supposedly failed and been kicked out when the Cultural Revolution came. I wondered what they had left behind, and what had happened to a country that had locked out the Gospel for 25 years. What would a church look like that had had no freedom to preach the Gospel or hold meetings, and had not been influenced by the West for so long? How many in the church had actually survived the persecution and imprisonment? What percentage of the population was Christian, in a country that comprised 25% of the world's population?

All these and many other questions began to intrigue me, and not only me. I found that there was more of a concern for China in Christians' hearts than for almost any other country. More people wanted to visit China than anywhere else it seemed. By 1979 and the advent of the liberalisation policy, information began to filter through about Christian pastors being released from prison and of millions of people coming to Christ.

All this information led me to believe that I would one day see China, and not only that, over a period of years, God confirmed this through the mouths of other people.

In 1985 I met a man called Ross Paterson, who had been a missionary in Taiwan, sent out by the fellowship of the late David Watson in York. He could speak fluent Mandarin and had also had some involvement in Hong Kong. I said to him, as casually as possible, that if he ever went to China I would like to go with him as I felt God had given me a promise that I would visit the land.

We met again at a later date and Ross said to me, "when are you going to China, Norman?"

"You just give me a date and I will go" I replied, much to his surprise.

"Well, I am going" he responded.

"Then I am coming."

This was in the early part of 1986. The trip was set up for late 1986 and I was to see yet another dream fulfilled.

The itinerary was to consist of travelling to Hong Kong, China and Thailand. I was to find myself moved by each of the countries that I visited, particularly by the work of some of the people we met and it was an experience never to be forgotten.

Hong Kong

The Church in Hong Kong is very divided over the charismatic issue. In fact, some would say it is now polarised into 'for' and 'against' camps. I was, however, particularly impressed by some of the people that I met, and the work they are doing.

David Wang of Asian Outreach is one of the foremost men in Chinese affairs. He has made repeated trips into China and has a lot of contacts with churches there. He is something of a personal dynamo and has actually seen people raised from the dead!

An American we met by the name of Dennis Balcombe leads a church in Hong Kong that is growing well. He speaks Chinese fluently and has totally adapted himself to the Chinese way of life, to the point of eating Chinese delicacies that many westerners would find hard to swallow, without a second thought! His church is actively involved in supplying literature into mainland China on a regular basis.

Jackie Pullinger's work is particularly well known outside of Hong Kong because of her book 'Chasing the Dragon'. Her work of rehabilitating drug addicts still continues, but is in a transition stage as 'church' is being built from those who came to surrender their lives to Christ. On Sunday afternoons alone, over two hundred gather for worship and teaching, and the congregation is cross-cultural and multi-racial. Jackie has managed to blend different peoples together into one expression of the Kingdom. Former heroin addicts will undoubtedly be leaders of the Church in the future.

I developed a tremendous admiration for her and all she is doing. Sadly, a number of organisations have attempted to muscle in and take over her work, but to date she has resisted all such moves.

She still has her Saturday evening meetings in the Walled City, where some 60,000 people live. We went along to one of these meetings, but once we were inside the City, I was glad I had not gone alone. It is a hang-out for alcoholics, drug addicts, prostitutes, opium dealers and the triad gangs, and everyone looks at you suspiciously. It is like a rabbit warren; a slum area of tenement blocks that are so close, it is almost as if they are joined together at the tops of the buildings. Numerous alleyways create a tunnel effect and the whole area is like a city within a city. As you walk down the streets, one thing is obvious; Jackie Pullinger is honoured, loved and respected for the work she is doing. Everyone else is not so welcome!

The small room where we met was given to her by the people of the area. 50 to 60 people were packed in for a meeting, and as Jackie began to speak in fluent Cantonese, the love and presence of God just seemed to flow out of her. The congregation was a mixture of new converts plus people they had brought in from the street, some stoned out of their minds, and others drunk. As Jackie did her Bible study, her compassion was obvious and I felt overwhelmed by the love of God that was evident in the room. At the end of her address, she asked people to respond, and six stood to accept Christ. New converts, not long saved themselves, began to pray for those who had stood. I could not cope with what was happening any longer and broke down and wept like a baby. I cried so much the people became concerned for me and started to pray for me. I felt like asking them not to, for God had touched me, and I was totally overwhelmed by the love of God.

In Hong Kong you can pay 1000 dollars a month for a flat. In recognition of her work the Government has given Jackie a disused refugee camp that is comprised of 12 Nissen huts, showers, toilets, a canteen, a workshop and a sports area. There is an endless stream of homeless people who want to come in and she cares for them all, feeding everybody who comes. In the office she has a file on the street sleepers, for whom she also cares. Her shepherd's heart is more than apparent as she cares for people such as these, as well as the homeless, drug addicts, displaced persons and down and outs, to name but a few. She is on call night and day, such is her love for the people.

Then she showed us into her own living quarters. It is a room 10ft x 8ft in which there is everything she possesses. A lady who has invites from all over the world to speak and tell of her work lives in such a room. To say that all of this is incredibly challenging, is surely the understatement of the decade.

As 1997 approaches rapidly and Hong Kong will be given back to Communist China, Jackie feels slightly pessimistic. She is not sure how much the Chinese can be trusted to keep some of the promises they have made. She is planning to break the Church down into small cell groups, meeting in homes, often in high-rise buildings, hoping that in this way the Body of Christ will be able to cope with whatever changes are brought about under a new regime.

China

On the 16th November 1986 Ross Paterson, Rodney Kingstone from Worthing and I went into China. We travelled 4 hours by train to Canton, the nearest city to Hong Kong, and stayed overnight in a hotel called the White Swan, which was certainly unashamed luxury for a communist state. The hotel's rooms were probably bugged, and we were very carefully watched by a lady on every landing who kept an eye on our comings and goings and monitored who entered and left the rooms. We were followed in the hotel and while we were out shopping.

China is certainly an enigma. It is definitely trying to liberalise in certain areas and superficially it appears open. Underneath the surface, however, it is still a controlled society. Christians are supposed to be accepted, but outside of the officially recognised state church, called the Three Self Movement, they are still harrassed and persecuted. You cannot talk openly and freely about the Lord to the Chinese, or even to one another. People are always listening in on your conversation. There is no concept of privacy or private property. The Three Self Movement has some genuine believers in it, both as members of the congregations and some pastors, but at the top it is definitely political and must follow the party line.

It is estimated that there are some 50,000,000 believers in China, and a high proportion of these meet in house group type situations, mostly in small gatherings. They are totally evangelical and often charismatic.

From Canton we travelled by train to Peking, a city of 10,000,000 where there are only 3 official churches. The train journey lasted 36 hours, six people to a compartment, sleeping on 3 bunks either side, with a 2ft 6in gap between bunks. By the time you had adjusted blankets and pillows and a space for luggage, there was very little room left for your body, especially as all the bunks were under 6ft long, and the three of us travelling together were a minimum of 6ft tall.

The regimentation that has become a part of the Chinese way of life was fairly obvious. At 10 p.m. a lady came along the train to switch out all the lights; a sign that it was expected of everyone to sleep - now! At 6 a.m. we were all woken up; there was no choice in the matter. That aside, however, the journey was not too unpleasant, although it was with some relief we reached Peking, having not been able to change our clothes for 36 hours.

Peking is just beginning to modernise. There is an excellent road system of four to six lanes width, with bikes everywhere. Hotels are beginning to spring up, the most famous among them being the Hilton and Sheraton Hotels. We never once saw what, for many in the West, are still the traditional symbols of China: the rickshaw and the coolie hat. Everybody wears blue uniforms except for members of the armed forces who wear brown decorated with red stars. China has the biggest army in the world, comprising between 8 to 10,000,000 soldiers. Everywhere you go there is a military presence and since all soldiers are communist party members, you have to be extremely careful what you say.

We stayed in a hostel in Peking where the temperature inside the building fairly accurately mirrored the below zero temperatures outside. After our long journey, the first thing we wanted to do was to take a shower, so we all made a bee line for the basement where the showers were located. Eagerly I turned on the shower, only to be hit full in the face by a jet of freezing cold water. "Oh no," I muttered. But I determined not to let it get me down. I prayed out loud, "I'll bless you for cold water Lord. I will give you thanks for it, but I would appreciate hot water." I could hear Ross and Rodney laughing. Just as I said these words, the water turned to hot. I do not remember praising God so loudly in English or in other tongues, and it certainly caused some hilarity for my travelling companions.

China's rapid moves to bring itself into the 20th century are certainly amazing, but they are also paying the price. The departed Mao Tse-tung is blamed for what is seen as a gigantic step backwards in Chinese history and the people are very angry about the Cultural Revolution. Mao was really in disgrace after his death and his mausoleum is still closed to the public, although he has been 'upgraded' again more recently.

The modernisation of society, however, is exacting its toll. Everyone is strongly encouraged to have only one child. Parents are required to pay tax penalties if they have two children and abortion, therefore, is a common occurrence in Chinese life. Although, at the moment, Christians are not so aware of the ethics involved, it will come more into focus for them as increasing amounts of literature become available from the West. Then it could become a real problem for the Church and heaven knows what the consequences of that might be! The additional problem is that girls are destroyed and boys are allowed to live; a truly horrendous situation. A further problem is that the one child in the family is totally spoilt and doted upon. The Chinese are besotted by their children and most of these kids are grossly overweight, so pampered are they. Many problems are being created for the future.

We moved on from Peking because we had been invited to speak at a University by a lecturer who was in charge of English studies and had spent some time in England. We arrived with the temperature still below zero, and found to our dismay the university had no heating in operation. This was, apparently, because the date had not yet arrived for switching on the heating, and whether the temperature outside was warm enough or not played no part in the decision to switch on the supply of warmth to the building. It reminded me of British Rail!

We were given a meal when we arrived. It was clear, very clear soup, with tree fungus and cabbage in it. As I sat there I could see a huge, square polystyrene container filled to the brim with MacDonalds junk food floating before my eyes. Sadly it was an illusion!

The subject we were given to speak on was 'The Relativity of the Christian Religion in England', which we gladly accepted as an opportunity to share our faith. It was extremely interesting talking to a class of students who have so obviously been processed educationally. When we spoke about scientists who believed in God and the Creation, they could not believe it, because they had been taught so differently and in a totally biased fashion. It was obvious, however, that the western influence was beginning to make its mark. There were three groups discernible in the class; those who had been processed and had not changed; those who were beginning to question and others who were already changing and opening up to new things. It was easy to tell which students belonged to which group, simply by the questions they asked. The time was very profitable and a rare chance for us to speak so openly of our faith in God.

From the University we travelled 18 hours by train to Shanghai, a famous old city which, of all the cities, had probably managed to stay the most traditionally Chinese in flavour. It is, however, rapidly becoming a modern city. While there we visited the original Tea House of 'The

Willow Pattern' and also went down to the famous Shanghai river where we saw Chinese junks moored alongside modern ships. If you are English, you could stand at the riverside all day long and have nothing else happen to you but a constant string of people talking to you, because they wanted to practise their English. There is little doubt that there are real opportunities for English teachers at the moment, for it is the language the Chinese want to learn the most.

There we met a remarkable man called Pastor Wang Ming Tao. He was imprisoned for 21 years for his faith. We visited him in the couple of rooms he had in a tenement block and talked about his time in prison, the suffering and the fears. He insisted on singing a song to us in English, the old favourite "All the way my Saviour leads me" which he sings with great gusto. He is now going blind and deaf. We asked him to pray for us, but he could not grasp that we would want him to do such a thing, such was his humility. We were whispering to him, but he was talking so loudly the whole block could have heard him.

We flew from Shanghai to Canton and met another Pastor called Lin. He had also been imprisoned for his faith, but since his release had baptised 900 people and reckons that 2,000 attend the house groups meeting in Canton. He has a few full time workers and the church is engaged in evangelism and church planting.

Five years before his release his wife died, so he never saw her again. He had a very high profile and international recognition. He even has an inscribed pen from President Reagan. He is clearly outspoken, but is not anti-government, only anti-State Church.

The man was an inspiration to us and we were deeply moved by our meeting with him. His words will remain etched in my memory and are a challenge to all of us - "I don't know how much time I have. I'm going to make it count!"

We left China clearly aware of certain needs. One doctor that we met has a vision for an old people's home. He said that it could be established for about £10,000 and would be run on Christian lines and a visible testimony of the love and care of Jesus to the community. It would serve retired full time servants of the Lord, some with little finance of their own. I certainly came home with this very much alive in my heart and am looking to see what can be done through Links International.

The obvious need in the Church is for good teaching material and leaders to be equipped for teaching and leading the people. Much could be done by way of encouragement to let the believers know they are not forgotten by the Church in the West.

Thailand

After a quick hop back into Hong Kong for 24 hours, we flew into Thailand and met up with two members of Team Spirit who were in the country, Dave Summers and Andy Au. Dave was a missionary in Thailand for a number of years, and although he now leads a thriving fellowship in Malvern, his concern for Thailand continues.

The whole of our time was spent in Bangkok at the Hope of Bangkok Church led by a Dr. Kriengsak. He is a brilliant man with a considerable intellect, very gifted administrator and no mean theologian. He went to Australia to study on a government sponsorship as a Buddhist, was witnessed to by a Christian and came to know Christ as Lord. He joined the Assemblies of God in Australia and led 500 people to the Lord in 2 years. He met a Thai woman in Australia who was a Christian, married her and returned to Bangkok. Feeling that his first priority in life was to preach the Gospel, he rented a room in a hotel for meetings and 17 people came to the first meeting. In 5 years the congregation has grown to

1,600 and needless to say, they no longer meet in a hotel room!

There is much emphasis on prayer in the church. Sundays begin with a 7.30 a.m. prayer meeting and there are early morning prayer meetings mid-week. They fill a disused cinema every Sunday, which is now not big enough for the congregations they are getting. Sunday is, in fact, a total workday for the Christians involved. Apart from the meetings, they have offices where they run their own Bible School, have English speaking classes, typing classes, and courses in art and design; they run their own clinic and in fact every Sunday is almost like a day's conference at one of the big Bible weeks in Britain. It is an incredible set-up which is very high powered but very successful.

Dr. Kriengsak's vision, which has been very successfully passed on to everyone in the church, from the youngest convert to the oldest member, is to plant a church in every district of Thailand by the year 2000. This will mean some 260 churches being planted. So far they have around 20 and are totally positive about attaining their goal. Everybody knows about the vision and is totally committed to bringing it to fulfilment. No matter what meeting you are in, the subject comes out in some way. They all know where they are going, what they are aiming for and are going with the vision. What a dream, and what a challenge to see such total commitment to it!

In spite of reservations we may have about the high level of organisation and apparent work orientation, during our three days in Thailand we were humbled by the grace of God so evident and the singular minded attitude and commitment of the brethren.

Lessons to be Learned

Our trip to these three eastern countries left a deep impression on us. We came away aware of opportunities that exist for people to serve churches and use their jobs as a vehicle for preaching the gospel. There are certainly open doors for small teams to go into these countries to serve and be exposed first hand to the needs and opportunities.

We were aware too, that unless the particular part of a church that we represented, that is the house churches, caught a vision for world vision, it would become increasingly spiritually incestuous. We must give away what we have received from God and allow the Holy Spirit to break down our parochial mentality. There are opportunities almost unlimited for everyone to be involved in promoting the Kingdom of God in the earth. Oh that we would catch the vision in the same way the the members of the Hope of Bangkok Church have done! Oh that we would remember the words of Pastor Lin and not be condemned, but challenged to pursue our dreams, to dream bigger dreams and see what God can do through people who are willing to risk everything for the sake of his Kingdom.

"I don't know how much time I have left. I'm going to make it count!"

Chapter 10
David's Tent

King David had a dream. As he sat in his palace his heart was moved because of the relative wealth surrounding him. He turned to Nathan the prophet and said, *"here I am, living in a palace of Cedar while the Ark of the Covenant of the Lord is under a tent."* (1 Chronicles 17 v 1).

Nathan did not think too much about what David said but simply encouraged him to do whatever he had in mind, fairly confident that God was with the king in what he planned to do. Then God spoke to him and said quite clearly that David was not the one to build a house for the Lord, but that his son would be the one to carry out the task.

David could have been downhearted, but along with this refusal by the Lord there were very many precious promises and so he was able to rejoice in the goodness of God. He did not sulk, he did not just forget the whole idea, instead he did what he could. He prepared the people for worship in the house of God.

David may have hit the depths at times in terms of his feelings and emotions, but he was undoubtedly a man of worship, and the preparations he made reflect his heart. In the first Book of Chronicles we read how he revolutionised and made worship central to the life-style of the nation. He appointed 4000 of the Levites just to be responsible for musical instruments with which to praise the Lord. He brought in singers, overseen by a chief singer, trumpet players to blow the trumpets regularly before the Ark of the Covenant, men and women who were not just expected to make a nice sound with their voices and instruments, but were expected to accompany prophecy and indeed prophesy on their instruments.

Such was the impact David's organisation made. Years

later in Israel's history, when Nehemiah returned to rebuild Jerusalem after the captivity and exile, one of the first things reintroduced upon completion of the practical work of rebuilding the city, was worship. We read these words in Nehemiah 12 v 45, 46. *"They perform the service of their God and the service of purification, as did also the singers and gatekeepers, according to the commands of David and his son Solomon. For long ago in the days of David and Asaph, there had been directions for the singers and for the songs of praise and thanksgiving to God."*

Worship reached new heights in Israel as a result of David's vision. In Acts 15 v 16, we read the following words, however. *"After this I will return and rebuild David's fallen tent."* This does, of course, refer to the fact that in David's tent gentiles were allowed to minister. A certain Obed-Edom, a Gittite, was asked to keep the Ark of the Covenant in his house (1 Chronicles 30 v 13), and as a result we find this man one of those appointed to minister to the Lord. But I believe it is more than that. David's tent was a place of rejoicing, worship and meeting with God and the verse in Acts 15 refers to the fact that God also wants to restore worship to its rightful place, right at the centre of the life of the Church.

Thankfully we are seeing a revival of worship in our generation. Men and women are being raised up by God to lead the people of God into new areas of worship. Gifted song writers are producing songs, hymns and choruses that express the heart of God for this moment in history, and praise and worship in many congregations is no longer merely the precursor to the 'more important' business of listening to the sermon.

Stateside Again!

On our last trip to Texas Grace and I became aware of the fact that in many of the churches we were visiting, although there was tremendous blessing and an overwhelming response to what we said, there seemed to be a limitation in the area of worship. There was singing, clapping and singing in the Spirit, but there seemed to be aspects that were lacking, particularly in the area of the prophetic. As a result of mentioning my concerns to some of the leaders and discussing ways in which we could help, it was agreed that we could take a team over to try and help develop things in the area of worship. We were going to try and do a bit of tent restoring!

Our team, apart from Grace and myself, consisted of musicians, dancers, a poet and a worship leader. We left London with the temperature in the 60's and arrived in Dallas/Forth Worth to be met by a heat of $90°$ plus. It was hot and remained so throughout the trip, on one occasion even reaching $107°$. Thank God for cold drinks and air-conditioning.

There was a real sense of expectancy and excitement when we arrived. I was thrown in at the deep end by the folks in Azle, our first stop. I started work at 6 a.m. in the morning at a prayer breakfast. Who said preachers have an easy life?

Our preparation for the trip had been quite rigorous and hard work, but it all seemed worthwhile when we began to see God move in the meetings. We started to move out prophetically, and one thing God showed us was that we could do this through music and dance, that is, to portray what he wanted to say through these vehicles. This was something that was new to all of us on the team, but God honoured us as we risked it. We called individuals or a couple out, prophesied and played music to them and then danced out the prophecy. Again and again God confirmed his word and at times the clarity of the words of knowledge and ministry were quite amazing.

One man in his early 40's, a big tall man, every inch a Texan with his jeans, boots and Texan belt, joined the drama team. I must confess I wondered what was going to happen, but when I saw him acting out a particular part, I was thrilled. He told me later that from the age of 17 he had wanted to do dancing, but there had been no opportunity to do it in the church.

How we have robbed people in the church of legitimate ways of expressing their love for God and of being able to bring God's word to us, through our narrow thinking. The Lord showed me clearly on the trip that dance, music and drama originated with him. It belongs to his Church. The world has stolen from us what is rightly ours. As I shared this with people, it was the means of release to many, when they began to understand that they were not being worldly but simply moving in areas that God wanted for them.

It was a real delight to see children who normally wanted to leave the meeting, stay and find excitement and a thrill in being able to dance, worship and bless the Lord. Many of the families wept over what God was doing among their children.

Our poetry, tap dancing, dancing, music and drama brought an enthusiastic response every time, and on our last evening the meeting lasted for 4 hours, with everyone finishing up weeping on each other's shoulders. We had been loved, cared for, spoilt and felt reluctant to leave, but it was on to Houston, via a short stay in Dallas.

We prophesied over one pastor in a town near Dallas, who had said he was totally against dance in the way we were portraying it, but after one of the women on the team danced, he said that he had no further doubt that such a thing was from God. The things that had been portrayed in the dance were exactly some of the things that were going on in his life and God spoke to him with absolute clarity.

It was a different kind of atmosphere in Houston, but God did some precious things among us. People began to realise that in God we could laugh and cry, stand or kneel, be still or dance, make a noise or be quiet, for it was all valid. Again the revelation that all these things belonged to God, and we were simply reclaiming what the Devil had stolen from us was a means of releasing many people.

After a visit to NASA the space centre, which has to be seen to be believed, we left Houston to travel 6 hours to Laredo and our good friends Norman and Sandra Howell.

The church has a large percentage of Mexicans, and as stated in a previous chapter, I always find it difficult to understand why they found it such a problem to move out in dance with all their background and ability. I began to realise, however, that there were many in the church who were middle-class Mexicans trying to forget their historical roots. On the Sunday morning we performed a play called 'Superfaith', after which Grace gave an appeal. As a result of this, 30 people came to the front and voluntarily prostrated themselves on the floor and wept deeply in the presence of God. It was a very moving occasion as we saw people touched by the Holy Spirit and families blessed.

Every night God did many good things among us. There were always people weeping and for the first time ever in the history of the church, everyone got out of their seats and danced together. At our last meeting we broke bread in a different way from the normal pattern of the church, with each person coming for some bread and taking it to others and using a communal cup as opposed to individual glasses. Again the Holy Spirit moved among us as people were reconciled and expressed commitment to one another. The music expressed the great variety that we have at hand to express our love for God and one another, moving from classical to country, to worship, with no gaps in between and no sense of 'this is sacred and this is secular music'. The process of regaining ground from the enemy continued!

On our last evening we were treated to a Mexican meal across the border in Mexico, with traditional players and singers on hand. The contrast between Mexico and the U.S.A. was vivid and a sobering reminder that two-thirds of the planet live like the Mexicans and not like their affluent neighbours.

Our next and last destination was Dallas, a 10 hour journey away. By the time we arrived we were pretty jaded and we found the meeting a little difficult right on top of such a journey. But we did see God break in, especially among the young people.

By now our thoughts were on home. When we eventually left we had many memories of lives touched and changed, fresh vision for a lot of people, swimming pools, hamburgers, cowboy hats, belts and boots, good friends and the ups and downs of operating as a fairly large team. I must confess that at times I wondered how to keep the 12 of us together properly. My deepest sympathies to Moses, how did he cope with millions in the desert?

Apart from all the blessing we saw and received ourselves, I believe that each member of the team came back with a fresh vision and new dreams to dream. Seeing God fulfil one dream inspires you to believe for others and so the process goes on, and God is able to bring about his purposes for our lives, and thrill and excite us along the way!

Chapter 11
Still Dreaming after all these Years

Many call Hebrews chapter 11 the faith chapter. It is not too difficult to see why. In many ways I would prefer it to be called the dreamer's chapter. In this glorious account of a number of people's lives, our eyes are opened to the possibilities for those who would hear the word of the Lord, allow it to take root in their hearts and minds, dream about it and by faith pursue it.

Noah was warned about the destruction of the world by a flood, dreamt about salvation through an ark and proceeded to make his dream reality, in the middle of the desert!

Abraham, well, we have already seen a lot of Abraham.

Joseph dreamt of a time when the people of Israel would again leave Egypt, and gave instructions for his bones to be taken with them when it happened.

Moses parents hid him when he as born, because they saw he was no ordinary child and dreamt of a significant future for him. And so I could go on, citing examples from this inspiring chapter. Men and women who, *"conquered kingdoms, and administered justice and gained what was promised."* These were ordinary people like you and me who believed God and pursued their dreams. Some of them met with ignominious deaths, but the dream in their heart was strong enough to enable them to face even that with courage and dignity.

After all that we have experienced in the past 20 years or so, it would be very tempting for Grace and I to sit back and think "it's time to take it easy." Thankfully, we are not like that. We are both still dreaming of new things to do, new projects to accomplish, new ways to serve the Lord. There appears to be no shortage of dreams!

In my study I have a world map with a pin stuck in every place in the world where I have stayed for at least one night. Every day I look at it, pray about it and ask the Lord where he would like me to go, and I encourage others to do the same.

David Mills and I have a dream of doing a tour of West Africa, using Church of Pentecost contacts, in order to see what is happening in countries like Nigeria, Liberia, Togo and Upper Volta. We want to try and gain a more exact overall picture of what God is doing in these countries.

As I look at the map, I see East Africa; Kenya; Uganda and Tanzania, and I am talking to God about those. I want to go and see them, just for the privilege of being there and seeing what God is doing.

Australia and New Zealand are coming into focus and I am certain that I will end up there before too long.

For years I have wanted to go to Afghanistan. In fact I am in competition with John Norton who also wants to go, to see who gets there first.

I have had three people speak to me about going to Russia. This is how God seems to deal with me. I have no particular longing to go there, but have a sneaky feeling that God will open up the way. I have, therefore, accepted the word and wait for God to do it.

Norman and Sandra Howell want us to go to Mexico to teach and preach at a Bible School. The Americans have a real emphasis on faith, from which we could learn something. Our emphasis is on community, sharing and relationships, all of which are very fragile in America.

Grace is still working on her dream of teams of women going to India, Africa and Mexico. She will begin in Ghana at the Biennial Women's Convention where there will be 50,000 women attending. Grace feels the conference will be a door-opener for her and the team that goes with her. She has a real concern for the women in these situations and wants them to know there are other women outside of their own situation who love them and care for them.

So many are the opportunities, that we are having to be more selective in what we get involved in. The blessing of God almost seems to bring its own problems. I was impressed when I met Derek Prince. He is a man of destiny who knows where he is going and also knows how to exercise patience and pace his life. I want to learn that. To be able to let go of the urgent for the important.

When I think back to my beginnings and those early prayer meetings in the Dagenham Elim Church, I realise that God has brought me a long way. The dream I had in my heart to reach the world was not an illusion, but something placed there by the Holy Spirit and in many respects I have seen that dream become reality. But I am not satisfied. Grace and I both feel an excitement about the future. God is the God of new things and we think that in many ways the best is yet to come. All that we have experienced of God gives us fresh faith for the future and we recommend to others the thrill of dreaming dreams, pursuing their hopes and aspirations, following the vision and putting their trust in the God who delights in making dreams come true.